This Is My Story; This Is My Song!

LULU ROMAN

If you're going to write your life story, chances are that there is one question that might cross your mind a time or two...or three.

That question is... what if no one buys it?!

As I pondered, "Who would want to buy my book? Who would get anything out of my life?", these are the answers I came up with.

If you were a fan of Hee Haw... that's a no-brainer (I probably shouldn't say "no-brainer" and Hee Haw in the same sentence! Ha!).

If you love Country or Gospel music, you should find lots of interesting things in my book.

But who else would get something from my life?

Have you ever had a loved one die? Someone you loved so much that you wanted to die too?

Have you ever messed up your life?

Have you ever questioned God and your faith?

Have you ever felt unloved or abandoned?

If you can relate to any of the above... then, have I got a story for you!

This is my story; This is my song!

– LULU

This Is My Story;
This Is My Song!

LULU ROMAN

The Autobiography

With Scot England

This Is My Story; This Is My Song! by LuLu Roman

ISBN: 978-0-9986367-4-0

Copyright 2019 England Media

Editor: Lindsey McNealy

Cover Design / Layout: Paula Underwood Winters

Cover Photo: Mary Elizabeth Long

My special thanks to the Hee Haw photographers including: Dean Dixon, Tony Esparaza, Marv Newton, Greg Zajack, Marshall Paulk, Jim Frey, Ralph Nelson and Harold McBroyen

www.luluromanbook.com Website Design: Katie Vickery
Printed in the United State of America

For more info on Lulu Roman, including her tour dates, latest CDS and other merchandise, visit www.luluroman.com
Published by:

England Media

102 Rachels Ct. Hendersonville TN 37075

(615) 804-0361

englandmedia@yahoo.com

If you enjoyed this book, you will also like these autobiographies published by England Media:

Ronnie McDowell "Bringing It to You Personally"

Johnny Lee "Still Lookin' for Love"

Moe Bandy "Lucky Me"

Jimmy Capps "The Man in Back"

DEDICATION

I dedicate this book to my Justin.

Baby, you were a mama's dream. You gave me unspeakable joy, and a heart full of smiles to make my days so memorable and my life so complete. We will see you soon when the sun rises over the rainbows.

–Mommy

INTRODUCTION

"From the very early years of my youthful career, through these days of waning ability, Lulu Roman has been an unexplainable constant in my life. She is an Angel on this Earth! Her infectious laugh and sweet smile permeate the space around her, and spread unknowingly, in spite of the obstacles, disappointments, and challenges she has had to overcome from the beginning. Lu inspires me!

The difference she continues to make in the hearts of those she touches, will live on with them always—and, they too will pass it on, just as she taught! The world is blessed by her life. Ms. Lulu's story is worth hearing and her Godly example is a large, but kind footprint to follow. I'm fortunate to be able to call her 'friend'… Forever and Ever, Amen!"

–Randy Travis

CONTENTS

Foreword   By Sharon White Skaggs & Lorrie Morgan xiii

Chapter 1   Orphan Girl 1

Chapter 2   Amazing Grace 13

Chapter 3   Operator, Can You Help Me Make This Call 19

Chapter 4   Finding Lulu...In Jail 23

Chapter 5   Sex, Drugs and...More Sex 29

Chapter 6   The Biggest Go-Go Dancer In Dallas Texas 35

Chapter 7   Hello Hee Haw 39

Chapter 8   Real Life Is No Kornfield Kounty 47

Chapter 9   From Jail to Jesus 55

Chapter 10   Lost and Found 63

Chapter 11   Sal-ute! 75

Chapter 12   Be Our Guest 93

Chapter 13   Gloom, Despair, and Agony on Me 99

Chapter 14   From My Dream Lover To a Nightmare 117

Chapter 15   A TV Star is Born 125

Chapter 16   A Littler Lulu 127

Chapter 17   Tammy and Dottie 133

Chapter 18   Justin 139

Chapter 19   Loving LuLu 145

Chapter 20   Old Friends...and a New Daughter 149

Chapter 21   Up, Up and Away! 155

Chapter 22   Parting Song 159

"My story will rock your world!"

Over the past five or six years, I have used that sentence many times, as people have asked me if I was going to write my autobiography. I knew my life story... the truth... was something that many of my fans (and some friends) would find almost unbelievable.

But little did I know that, before I would get this book finished, it would be MY world that was truly rocked... like never before. My son died.

For months, I couldn't have cared less if I ever completed my book. As far as I was concerned, my book might not have been done... but I was. I couldn't go on without him.

But then something happened. I did go on.

The process of writing an autobiography is not easy. You really have to be willing to pour out your heart, and it's a lot harder when your heart is breaking. I have had such wonderful moments in my life. But I have had just as many heartbreaks.

Who knows... maybe one of the reasons I did go on was so that I could get this book to YOU. That seems to be a pretty deep thought, for the fat girl from Hee Haw, but you're about to find out that I have always been a lot deeper than most people knew.

FOREWORD

"The first time I met Lulu Roman, I was struck by what a warm, friendly and enthusiastic person she was. She was so full of life and energy... and she still is! I had been a fan of hers long before we'd ever met in person. My family had watched Hee Haw for years, and when the Whites and my husband, Ricky Skaggs, were asked to be on the show, it was a very big deal for all of us. We were all nervous, but Lulu made us feel very welcome.

It's hard to believe now that almost forty years have passed since that first meeting. But over the past four decades, Lulu has become one of my closest and dearest friends. I am blessed to have many friends in the music and entertainment industry, but my friendship with Lulu is a much deeper kind of friendship than most of those. She is more than a friend to me. She is family.

When my son Luke was born thirty years ago, Lulu came to visit. I was having a hard time getting Luke to sleep; he just cried and cried, and I was getting worn out. But as soon as Lulu walked in, she scooped him up and held him tight to her chest, and he went right to sleep. She had a way with him. And my kids still love her today. I also loved Lulu's sons. When her son Justin passed away, Ricky and I and the Whites sang at his funeral. We were so honored to do that for her.

Lulu is such a strong Christian. Our faith in Christ has strengthened the love and bond that we have for each other. We've gone to prayer meetings together, and we've done a lot of different events and benefits together. She has always been such a giver, and she's always been willing to help out any time someone asks her.

I will never forget one mission trip we took to Acuna, Mexico thirty years ago. We took a couple busloads of people there from Nashville; Barbara Fairchild helped put it all together. Lulu was there, and Ricky and I brought along our kids, along with my mom and dad. We ministered to the Mexican people who were living in true poverty. We shared the gospel with everyone there. Lulu sang and gave her testimony, and it was very powerful.

In 1988, my husband Ricky and I recorded a gospel song with Lulu called "Two More Hands". We were all a little surprised at how great it turned out, but it was a tremendous song. It ended up being a big hit. Lulu gave a great performance on that song. She is the real deal, as a singer and as an entertainer. It was a big thrill for me to get to sing with her on a record. It was a great blessing for me to be a part of that.

Lulu Roman is extremely talented. She can also connect with the crowd on many levels. Of course she is a great comedian... but when she shares her heart, the audience can feel her honesty. She relates to people in a very special way. She is so full of love.

I am so proud to be a part of Lulu's book, but I am even more proud to be a part of Lulu's life. She is a special part of the life of Ricky Skaggs and the Whites."

– Sharon White Skaggs

FOREWORD

"I grew up watching Lulu Roman on Hee Haw. I sat in front of the TV and watched her every week. To me, Lulu was a real TV star, and I still remember the first time I got to meet her in person. I was so excited! I was in awe. I couldn't believe I was meeting Lulu Roman!

When I was asked to be a guest on Hee Haw, it was such a surreal moment for me. After watching the show on TV when I was a kid, here I was now, actually stepping onto the set! I ended up doing Hee Haw a half dozen times, and during those shows, I found out that Lulu could sing so well. I was blown away. She is such a good singer.

I've gotten to work with Lulu a few times in the past couple of years, and she is a real special lady to work with. Lulu and I did a live tribute to the Hee Haw show in Nashville, and I hardly recognized her, after she had lost so much weight. She looked amazing.

As I got to know Lulu as a person, I was able to see the way that she lives her life. She is a wonderful Christian woman, and is so dedicated to the Lord. I respect her, and I am proud of what she has done with her life. I am honored to be her friend.

I know that Lulu loves to zipline, and I would love to go ziplining with her! That would be such a blast. But for now, I will just enjoy her book. I know that you will, too."

– Lorrie Morgan

ORPHAN GIRL

I came into this world as a bastard child.

How's that for a great way to start a book?! Probably not the best way to kick things off. It wasn't the greatest way to start off my life either. But I had no choice.

I was born in Pilot Point, Texas on May 6, 1946, in a home for unwed mothers. Ironically, the home was called "Hope Cottage". And to make things even worse, my unwed mother named me Bertha! Bertha Louise Hable. I have no idea where the name "Bertha" came from, I just knew that I hated it. So, I always went by my middle name, which was Louise.

As I look back on it now, I think, "Who names their kid Bertha? My mom must have been crazy!"

And she really was. Soon after giving birth to me, my mother was committed to Terrell State Hospital. She had been beaten and physically abused by most of the men in her life, and I assume one of those great guys was my father. I never knew who my dad was. My mom never offered up his name.

And I never offered up the name of "mom" to my mother. She never acted like a mother to me. So I always used her name of Clara Gene.

Her mother, my grandma, was even worse. There is no way I would call her "grandmother". I called her Claudine. If she wasn't the Devil, she at least knew him pretty well. She treated me so horribly. I can still hear her yelling at me, "You are a little piece of s--t!" Then she'd say, "No, that's not right. You are a big piece of s--t!" I still fight with that feeling of being unworthy, even today. Thanks Claudine.

I felt so unloved, and so unwanted, and so unworthy. You could call me the "un" girl. Claudine never missed a chance to tell me, "You are fat. You are ugly. And no one will ever love you." Imagine your grandmother telling you that... every day. It would do a number on you. I still have trouble with my self-esteem. I still hear the hateful words of my good ol' worthless grandmother. At times, those memories lead me to be my own worst enemy. I sometimes feel ugly, and don't even want to get out of bed.

Claudine had a good job with Holiday Inn of America. She was the Executive Innkeeper for the company, and everyone she worked with just loved her. They thought she was so wonderful. They had no idea how she treated me. A few years ago when I went back to Dallas, one of her former co-workers came to meet me, and I asked her if Claudine ever mentioned me. I was totally shocked when she said, "You are all she talked about! She was so proud of you."

I broke down into tears right then and there. What I wouldn't have given to have been able to hear my grandma tell me that she was proud of me.

My most vivid memory of Claudine is of her smoking one Camel cigarette after another. She wouldn't even let the first one go out before lighting the next one. She would always have one of those dirty cigs hanging from the side of her mouth as she cussed me out. Her horrible words were even worse than her horrible smell. And I'm absolutely sure that the smell of her cigarettes is the reason I never smoked. I didn't want to be anything like her.

Before I get any deeper into this book, I also need to first mention a book that came out more than forty years ago. It was supposed to be my autobiography. I don't know why I needed one back then... I was only in my early 30s!

As soon as that book was released, I hated it. I was totally embarrassed. It was full of made-up stories and complete lies, and for some reason, it barely mentioned Hee Haw!

But the worst thing about that book was the wonderful picture it painted of Claudine. At the time, I was still desperate to gain Claudine's love, so I told the world how blessed I was to have her in my life. I even started it off with a dedication: "To Claudine, my beloved grandmother, who was always there for me, no matter how many times I let her down. She is the world's greatest grandma and I love her more than words can ever tell."

When I read those lies today, I want to throw up! I hope none of those books still exist today.

We've all heard the old saying, "Sticks and stones may break my bones, but words will never harm me." What a total lie that is! Whoever came up with that crap was never a little girl who had to listen to their mother and grandmother tell them how worthless they were. Yeah, cussing out a three year old every day sure does harm them.

There is only one reason I survived my childhood: God. God was with me. I didn't know it then, but when I finally realized it, I also found out that God's love is unconditional, and I know I am beautiful to Him. Years ago, when I looked in the mirror, I believed my grandma. But she was a liar! And I want to tell anyone who is reading this book… God loves you! You are beautiful. And if you happen to be fat… fat is not an issue with God. Please know that you are beautiful in God's eyes. I sure wish that I had had somebody to tell that to me when I was growing up. It would have saved me a lot of heartache.

As I look back on things now, and as I still wonder who my father was, I have come up with a pretty disturbing possible answer. I'm not sure, but I really think that Claudine's husband, Fred (who I called PaPa), might have been my father. It had to be that my grandpa was also my father. I think maybe that's why Claudine was always angry at me, from the time I was a little girl. She was always very ugly to me.

Since my mother was mentally ill, and my grandma hated me, and with no father in my life, the burden of raising me was put onto my great grandmother. I called Great Grandma Imogene "Granny", and I thought she was wonderful. Granny was a lot nicer than Clara and Claudine, and she always made sure I was clean and that I looked nice. I can still hear her saying, "Cleanliness is next to Godliness." She really loved me. But her love also led to my love of sugar. She would put me on her knee, and as she'd rock me, she'd feed me cookies. She was always baking cookies or cake for me.

Granny was a short woman, but she had a very big heart, and she did the very best she could with me. But the burden of caring for a little girl soon became too great for her. One day, while Granny was at work, Claudine took my hand and announced, "We're gonna take a little drive."

On Friday, November 17, 1950, Claudine drove little Bertha Louise Hable to the Buckner Orphan's Home in Dallas, Texas. I thought we were walking into a hospital. Everything was totally white. The walls, the floors, the furniture, the uniforms of the workers, everything was white. And I tried to listen, as Claudine quietly talked with some women who looked like nurses. Then I tried to figure out why she was walking out the door… without me! I was four years old.

I passed the next few hours playing with the other children who were there. I had fun, and I couldn't wait to tell Grandma Imogene about all the new friends I had made. I'd tell her, as soon as Claudine came back to get me… but she never came back.

As darkness fell, one of the "nurses" told me to get ready for bed. When I responded, "My grandma will be coming to get me," she responded with a stern "Your grandmother is gone. She's not coming back. This is your home now."

Of course, I started crying, and then screaming. I really could have used a nice, big hug right then. But instead, the "nurse" grabbed me, turned me over her knee and spanked me.

She took me into a large room that had ten beds in it. Five were lined up along one side of the room, with five more on the opposite side. The woman threw me into one of those beds with, "I'll blister your bottom again if you make a sound!"

My little heart was crushed. I had been abandoned, and as tears rolled down my face, I wondered what I had done to make my family leave me there, and make me feel like I'd been thrown away.

I didn't sleep much that night. My eyes were wide as saucers, as my young mind tried to figure out all the new and scary sounds coming from all around me, from different parts of the home. I also listened to other children quietly weeping. But at some point, I did fall asleep… just long enough to wet the bed. The next morning, I received my second spanking, as the "nurse" yelled about the mess I had made.

The day they put me into the orphan's home, food became my comfort. Sugar became my friend. Sugar didn't call me names. It didn't put me down. But sugar also led to me being a fat kid, and I found out that no one wanted to adopt a fat kid. Buckner would be my home for the next fourteen years.

There were only two ways to leave the orphan's home: you either got adopted, or you stayed there until you graduated high school. That last one would be me. I was a long-timer.

The Buckner home had anywhere from 600 to 1,500 kids at a time. Most of the kids were throwaways. They weren't true orphans. It wasn't like our parents were dead. They were alive!

Most of us came from broken homes, or from a family that couldn't, or wouldn't, care for us.

We were just kids that nobody wanted. And when I got old enough to realize that, I was so embarrassed and ashamed. I lived my first eighteen years knowing that there was NO ONE out there who wanted me. You have no idea what that does to a person's self-esteem. It destroys it.

Speaking of destroying your self-esteem... on a regular basis, a nurse would come into our dorm and "check us for worms". We were made to pull down our panties and bend over, and if they happened to find something that looked odd to them, they would make us drink this horrible medicine, which almost instantly had us running for the toilet. They also checked every child for lice on a regular basis. They always seemed quite surprised when it turned out we didn't have any.

For many people, when you say the word "orphanage", they think of the Broadway musical or movie "Annie". Well, let me tell you, Annie didn't know how great she had it! She didn't get cussed-out and beaten every night. Some of our house mothers would have also beaten Annie's dog, just before taking it from her. Yeah, I don't remember any of us kids happily singing, "The sun will come out tomorrow!"

Most people have memories of their father or mother, memories of vacations or loving moments, or even a silly expression their parents might have said. But I had nothing. What I wouldn't give to have known of just a few moments of what it was like to have a family around me. I can only imagine what Christmas must be like if you have parents to sit with, and parents who express their love to you.

Almost from the time I drew my first breathe, the enemy was after me. God has a plan for everybody. But the Devil knows what that plan is, and he will try to stop it.

I was diagnosed with a serious thyroid problem when I was two years old. I had a non-functioning thyroid. I was sick most of the time, and I also had lots of allergies. My thyroid condition led to me being a pretty big girl, even at a very young age. And don't forget my comforter… sugar. I thought that cookies, chocolate cake and ice cream might make my pain and loneliness go away. It never worked, and I developed an addiction to food. Yes, little Bertha Louise was on her way to quickly becoming Big Bertha.

Now that I look back, I see that I really wasn't that big. But I was still bigger than all the other girls.

During my first year at the home, a boy named Jerry and I both got into major trouble. We were both four years old, playing in a sandbox outside. Jerry was the first friend I made at the home. He was a very sweet boy, with blue eyes and blonde hair. One day, as we played, we both pulled down our pants so we could "compare our parts." When a housemother saw us, we were both severely punished.

Jerry and I stayed in touch over the years. I always thanked him for being my friend when I really needed one, and we always laughed when we thought about that day back in the sandbox. Years later, Jerry died from AIDS, and when I got the news, I was heartbroken.

The Buckner Orphanage was a religious home. It had a strict religious atmosphere, with an emphasis on "strict". I say it was brutally Baptist.

We listened to Bible stories over and over. We were made to memorize scriptures. They served us God and religion for breakfast, lunch and dinner. They basically tried to shove God down our throats. I hated it all.

I always thought, "When I grow up and get out of here, I won't have to do any more of this Bible stuff." I never stopped to realize that what they were teaching us was going to take root in my spirit.

When I was in the First Grade, I got my first taste of stardom. We put on the play "Hansel and Gretel", and since I was one of the biggest girls (and I guess scariest), I played the wicked witch. I loved every minute of it! When I was reciting my lines, I could "become" the witch. And there, for a few minutes, I didn't have to be a scared, lonely little fat girl in an orphan's home.

My best friend in the orphan's home was Peggy Deleene. When we were kids, we would listen to polka music together and we'd dance all around the room. As I was writing this book, Peggy died from brain cancer. It broke my heart.

Each Saturday, all of the children in the orphanage had to do yard work. We would have to mow the yards, weed and trim the hedges. I was allergic to grass, along with almost every plant. I had allergies and asthma so bad. We all worked hard, and I always looked forward to our breaks, when they'd bring in a truck full of watermelons. They'd dump them on the ground, and we'd cut them in half and dive in. That was one little bit of pleasure I remember.

If we got all our work done on Saturday, they would show movies for us later that evening, in a theater under the church. They were mostly Westerns. We watched a lot of Randolph Scott movies. But one time, they played The Creature from the Black Lagoon. It scared me to death! And for many nights afterwards, I was afraid the Creature was hiding under my bed. I just knew that he was going to get me.

But even the Creature wasn't as scary as some of the people who worked there in the home. Many of the workers were only there for the paycheck; they weren't qualified to work with children, and that led to lots of abuse. Some really were monsters.

We received beatings on a regular basis. If we ever did something to get into trouble at church, we were extremely abused. They'd whip you with a leather strap. They'd lean us across our bed. One person would sit on our legs, while another would just beat the crap out of us.

Some of the housemothers had thick wooden paddles, with holes cut in them so that they would leave big welts on your bottom and legs.

I need to say, however, that not all of the teachers and housemothers there were bad. There were a couple who were very kind to me. But they were overshadowed by the ones who had no idea of how to properly take care of children.

To keep hundreds of children in line and on schedule, the orphanage used bells and whistles. Each morning, we would awaken to the sound of five very loud whistles. The first and second whistles were for the girls who had to get up at 5:30 to walk across campus and start making breakfast in Manna Hall. The third and fourth whistles were for the girls who would serve the food. The fifth and final whistle signaled that it was time for all of the other kids to form a double line to walk to the cafeteria.

The bells and whistles kept all of the kids in order. They also signaled when it was time for us to move from one class to another. Those bells and whistles sounded throughout the day, every day of the year, including on weekends and in the summer months. By the time I got out of that orphanage, I never wanted to hear another bell or whistle again!

There was one whistle that I almost never heard, though. That was a sports whistle. I was the last one ever chosen for any sports or games. I was always left out of everything. I was picked on and made fun of. And when the other kids saw that their teasing hurt me, they decided to kick it up a notch. Who could really blame them? They were all throwaways too. They had never had any love, and now they had found someone they could hurt in return. Every day, I got to hear "Fatty, Fatty, two by four... can't get through the kitchen door!"

If I was as smart back then as I am now, I would have told those mean kids, "Obviously, I DID get through the kitchen door... and I got something good and you didn't!"

But during that time, I found that I could use my sense of humor as a defense when the other children were teasing me. I found that I had a talent to make a funny face, or to act silly, and the other kids would laugh WITH me instead of AT me. If I was already laughing at myself, they didn't find it as fun to put me down. That ability to make people laugh became a security blanket for me, and at a very early age, I told myself, "When I grow up, I want be a comedian."

I loved music, even as a young girl. I jumped at the chance to take piano lessons, and after my first few sessions, my teacher told me she thought I had some talent. But no matter how hard I practiced, there was one other girl who was always much better than me. However, I discovered a skill that she didn't have… I could play "Chopsticks" with my toes!

The girl begged me to show her how to do it too. We both lay back on the piano bench, and I demonstrated how to arch my back so that I could put my toes up on the piano. Right then, one of the housemothers walked in, jerking us both off of the bench. That was the last of my piano lessons… something I deeply regret to this day. People always like to ask, "Is there anything from your life that you regret?", and that is the one thing. Me getting in trouble that day robbed me of getting to continue taking piano lessons. I know if I had continued the piano, I would have been able to write music.

My most memorable Valentine's Day as a young girl came when I gave a valentine to a boy I liked. I had worked a long time on the card, making sure that it was just perfect. In return, he gave me a valentine that made fun of me being fat.

We had a school on the campus meant for younger kids, but when we got older, they sent us to a public high school. We had to take a bus that had huge letters plastered on the side that read "Buckner Orphan's Home".

We felt so horrible stepping off of that bus. All the students from the Samuell High School were watching us. They knew we didn't have any parents, and they started making fun of us almost the moment we arrived. Each day they would yell out: "Here come the orphans!" and "Hey Orphan Annie!"

To make things even worse, they called our bus "Big Bertha". They named it that because it was big and ugly. Of course, Bertha was also MY name. My below-ground self-esteem went even lower.

But there were a few bright spots during my teenage years. Even though I was quite large, I was a great swimmer. I loved swimming, and no other student could beat me in the backstroke, not even the boys! Even at 200 pounds, I could float on top of the water for 45 minutes at a time. I became such a good swimmer that I became certified as a Red Cross lifeguard.

Usually, my favorite subject in school would have been lunch, but they gave all the orphan kids a special card that we would pay with. That card showed the lunch lady that we didn't have any money. My friend Peggy would never even eat lunch, because she was too embarrassed to show that card.

In high school, I took a speech class, and it involved public speaking. Of course, I didn't yet realize that that class was helping to prepare me for things that would come later in my life. I was in the concert choir, and performed in operettas and plays, and those all led to my chance to experience some kind of intimacy. While I was doing those musicals, I learned how to French Kiss with a boy behind the bleachers.

My first real kiss was with a boy named Jimmy. He was a really cute guy from off campus. He drove a big blue convertible. He was sweet, and he loved to kiss me! Jimmy never spoke to me like most other boys did. He never called me "fat". I adored him, but we never went farther than kissing.

During my senior year, I got into trouble for "necking" backstage during our play rehearsals. Several of us would go under the choir risers and "practice our kissing technique". When a teacher caught us, they called us "thugs".

In one of the musical productions, I played Hattie the Maid in "Kiss Me Kate". And I actually sang a couple things in it. My singing wasn't that great, but I was very loud! I could project my voice from the stage all the way to the back of the auditorium.

I never looked at myself as a singer, but I was the only person who could ever hit that note they wanted at the end of the concerts, ya know the one where they say, "It ain't over till the fat lady sings"? Yeah, I could always hit that one.

AMAZING GRACE

One of my friends in the orphanage was a boy named James Ryle. James' life after the orphanage was far from easy, and I was sad to learn that he ended up in prison. As I thought of him behind bars, I remembered when we attended all the church services at the orphan's home. James always seemed to pay much more attention to the sermons than I did.

James was listening to those messages, and he was able to use his faith to turn his life completely around, as he became a remarkable man of God. In the years after his release from prison, James went on to become a wonderful pastor! He pastored the Boulder Valley Vineyard in Boulder, Colorado, and he was also a chaplain for the Denver Broncos football team.

James ended up helping to start the Promise Keepers men's ministry. And back when we were in church together, James would actually sing when we were told to sing "Amazing Grace". I just sat there and mouthed the words.

I had no idea what Amazing Grace meant. I didn't know what it meant when I was a young girl. I just knew that my life had been far from amazing, and I spent a large part of my adult life searching for its meaning. But then my friend James told me that he knew the meaning of Grace, and he gave me this wonderful definition. He said, "Grace is the empowering presence of God in our lives. That enables us to be who He has called us to be… so that we can do what He has called us to do… right where we are."

I live by those sentences today. I wish my mom had been able to feel the presence of God. But she didn't.

My mother was in the Terrell mental institution most of the time that I was in the orphan's home. Everyone always said it was the "Coo-Coo House". Claudine had told me that the reason mom was in the institution was that she had something called pyelitis, and it had fried her brain. I later found out that pyelitis was a problem with the kidneys, and not the brain. Many years later, I asked my Aunt Edna about Claudine's explanation, and she said it was not true. She said my mother got brain damage from being hit in the head with a skillet and bottles when she was a young girl.

Clara Gene (my mom who I refuse to call mom) ran away from the institution a number of times. On one occasion in the late 60s, she ran away and met a soldier on a bus. His name was Leonard, and she ended up marrying him! Leonard was an alcoholic, but they loved each other, and he took care of her.

One day, Clara Gene and Leonard came to see me at the orphanage. I was a Senior in high school at the time, and I hadn't seen my mother for many years. As soon as I saw them walking across the campus, I knew that they were finally coming to take me home. I was almost a grown woman, but I figured "better late than never." But as I watched them get closer, I noticed Leonard was carrying a special gift. I was immediately mortified! My gift was a five-foot-tall doll. I was so embarrassed. I was almost 18 years old! I suppose mom had told her husband about her "little girl", so he'd figured I would want a doll. I have no idea if Clara Gene even knew how many years I had been locked up inside that place.

As we said our hellos, I thought I should just forget about the five-foot-tall doll. I could always leave it behind as they took me home. But I quickly found out that, not only would the doll be staying behind... but so would I. My mother had not come to take me out of the orphanage. She had come to break my heart one more time. They had come to tell me goodbye. They were moving to Germany.

Clara Gene and Leonard stayed married until his death. When he died, they put his body in the back of a pickup truck and drove him to Little Rock, Arkansas, where he was buried.

At the orphan's home, we never heard "I love you." We never heard "You are going to make it." We were never told "You can do what you want to with your life." We never got any kind of affirmation. I had no one to even teach me right from wrong. I had no father to pick me up and love me when I needed a hug. Boy, did I need a hug.

With no hugs coming back then, I ran away to music. I had a little, plastic radio, and I hid it under my bed. At night, all of the girls would lie down on the floor and listen to that radio. When I got older, I would wear earphones, and I'd lie on the floor and listen to hard rock music. Today, music is still my cave that I can run into to be alone and enjoy the cool air. Today, I listen to soul and rhythm and blues gospel music.

I did learn a lot of life skills in the orphanage. I studied typing for six years, and I took Home Economics for seven. They taught us how to sew and cook. I became a very good cook, thanks to the skills I learned in the orphan's home. As part of my training, I was assigned to work in the home's kitchen. I'm pretty sure that those operating the orphanage found that, not only could this be a learning experience for the kids, but it also saved them money, because they didn't have to pay an adult cook to come in!

I spent my entire first day in the kitchen peeling potatoes. I peeled those potatoes until I couldn't even bend my fingers anymore. They were almost bleeding. When I commented that I thought I had cut enough to last a week, one of the cooks said, "That won't even get us through dinner!" You try peeling enough potatoes to feed 1,500 kids! Your hands will bleed too!

When I worked in the kitchen, I had to get up extra early so that we could get started making breakfast. I dreaded being the first one in the kitchen, because the one who turned on the lights was also the one who got to see the overnight rats scurry away. Those rats were huge!

The meals at the home were a big production, just because they had so many kids to feed. We ate at what was called Manna Hall, a huge room that seemed the size of a football field. It had to be big, because each meal they fed 800-1,500 kids. We ate three meals a day there. Every Junior and Senior girl was assigned a table. We went into the kitchen and got food for our table, and then served everything to the younger kids. We poured the drinks, and then after the meal, we cleaned each table.

When I wasn't working in the kitchen, I was helping in the school library. I also worked in the orphanage laundry. Most of my time there was spent washing and drying bed sheets.

During our teenage years, we learned different occupations that we might go into once we left the home. My favorite class was Cosmetology. We learned hairdressing skills there, and I always looked forward to the days we got to practice with makeup and hair color. I loved changing my hair, and I went from blonde to red to brunette almost every week.

I am a natural strawberry blonde. I really am! But by the time I got on Hee Haw, I had already turned my hair pink and blue and red and green. When Hee Haw started, I just happened to be dyeing my hair dark black. I had very long pig tails, all my own hair. No one with the show told me how to do my hair. That was just me, and how I wore my hair at the time.

But there was one thing I couldn't understand. We were being trained in how to properly apply makeup to customers if we became beauticians, but almost every Sunday, the preacher in the orphan's home would yell at us, "Do not paint your face like a street walker!"

That same preacher also warned us from the pulpit, "Do not dance. Don't talk to no niggers and don't talk to no Catholics!" I guess I ended up doing just about everything that preacher told me not to do. I never was a very good listener!

I can say that all of us kids did learn some important life skills at the orphan's home, but when they sent us out to public high school for our Sophomore, Junior and Senior years, about the only thing I learned… was how to do drugs. I found out that if I took drugs, I could get high enough to get away from the ugliness of my life. I was a drug addict by the time I was 16 years old.

I left the orphan's home with a very angry spirit. I was very mad at God. I knew that there was a God. I had no doubt about that. But that made me even angrier. I knew He was there, and He was in charge of everything. So why did He allow me to go my entire life without a mom and dad? Why did He make me be alone, with no one to love or care about me?

There are no answers for my questions here on Earth. I know I will have to wait until I can get in God's face so I can ask him, "What were you thinking?! Did you think that I was strong enough to carry the weight of the world on my shoulders?"

I'm sure all that pain that I felt is why I turned into such a good actress. Me being the silly woman who made everyone laugh, that was how I could cope with everything that I had to live through. And if I'd thought I had it rough during my first 18 years… my troubles were only just beginning.

OPERATOR,
CAN YOU HELP MAKE THIS CALL?

There is one day during my teenage years that I remember more than all the others. It was a day that I skipped school. But I had a very good reason… I wanted to see the President.

On November 22, 1963, I went with my friends Peggy and Marilyn to downtown Dallas. We had heard that President Kennedy would be passing through, and we wanted to try and catch a glimpse of the young and handsome leader we were all in love with.

The three of us got there a little bit early, and we were able to get a good spot right by the Texas School Book Depository building. That's exactly where I was, when the President's motorcade came down Houston Street. We got an even closer look at Mr. Kennedy, as his car made a left turn onto Elm Street. We were so happy to be there! We were sure he was waving right at us!

Then it all came to an end.

I heard three shots. I looked at Peggy and Marilyn. We didn't know what was happening. Everyone started running. As we tried to keep up with the motorcade, we saw a man running up what is now called the grassy knoll. He had blonde or light brown hair, with a buzz haircut. He was wearing a Seersucker suit and he was carrying a rifle. We never found out if he was trying to escape, or if he was a policeman, running toward the suspected shooter.

Anyone who was alive at the time can tell you exactly where they were when John Kennedy was assassinated. I know I will never forget where I was. I had a front row seat.

Just before we had left the orphanage, all the graduating boys were told to apply for work at the local power company. Most of the girls were sent to the Southwestern Bell Telephone Company. They gave us six weeks of training on the telephone switchboard there. We practiced plugging cords into different holes, as we connected each call.

Remember the old Laugh In skit where Lily Tomlin was the telephone operator? She wore a headset and moved around all the phone cords, as she said, "One ringy dingy..." That was me! I would work as a telephone operator for the next two and a half years.

While I was in the orphan's home, I came up with a short bucket list of things I wanted to do as soon as I got out on my own. One of those things was, I wanted to learn how to cuss! And I quickly mastered that! I got it down very fast! For some reason, I was just attracted to curse words. Maybe it was because the school was so strict about everything... but if they had a class for cussing, I would have become the valedictorian.

But my fondness for foul words proved to be a small problem on the very first call I took as a telephone operator. When I picked up and said, "Operator", a British voice said back, "I would like to place a call to Ringo Starr."

I yelled into my mouthpiece, "You've got to be sh!tin' me!"

Anytime someone would call the operator and say something rude (which was about every other call), I would just say something rude right back at them. If they cursed at me, I would cuss right back at them. Sometimes I would cuss them out even before they got me!

My bosses were always telling me that I was not allowed to use bad language to my callers. But I had become a union steward for the company, so it took them a couple years before they could fire me. One day, though, the boss came to me, carrying a big paper tablet. They had written down everything that I had said over the past two and a half months. Those tablets were filled with many pages of some pretty impressive and entertaining stuff!

When my boss told me I was fired, I threw down my earphones, and I threw them so hard that they broke into a dozen pieces. Then, with every step I took toward the door, I said a new cuss word to the boss.

I found it ironic that after all of my cussing on the job, Ma Bell was now telling me where to go! Many years later, I laughed to think that they let Irlene Mandrell play the telephone operator on Hee Haw and not me! Maybe they had heard stories of my time at that phone company!

FINDING LULU… IN JAIL

We learned to never get attached to our room in the orphan's home. Each summer, all of the kids would be moved onto a different floor, or even into a different building on campus.

When you first came into the home, if you were a young child like I was, you were sent to a building called the Sunbeam Home, a place for newborn babies and children up to the age of four. When you went to First Grade, you were moved to the Harding Building. When you got to the Third Grade, you moved to another building, and as we got older, we just continued moving to different buildings.

The main reason for the revolving and ever-changing rooms was because when the Senior students graduated high school each year, they were ushered out of the orphanage and sent off into the "real world". Junior and Senior students shared a building called Pender Hall, and when the Seniors left, the Juniors who had been on the second floor of the building would then move to the bottom floor.

This huge moving process took place every summer. Everybody made some kind of move, as we worked our way around all the buildings that sat in a big circle on the campus.

I graduated from W.W. Samuell High School on May 28, 1964. Like all the other poor kids, the moment I finished the 12th Grade, I was escorted out of the Buckner Orphan's Home. They gave me a suitcase and $50.00, and sent me out into the real world. Luckily, I wasn't completely alone. My friend Peggy had also just graduated. We had both been best friends from the time we'd been put in the home. And our friendship would continue as we became adults.

We got an apartment together. I still remember the address… 3416 Bryan St., #205. For our first dinner, we cooked spaghetti and baked potatoes, and we celebrated our newfound freedom by yelling, "No one can yell at us anymore! No one can tell us what to do!"

But our celebration didn't last long. We were about to find out that we had moved into the very roughest part of Dallas, Texas!

The first night in our apartment, my diamond ring and watch were stolen. They had been my grandmother's. In the next few weeks, our apartment was broken into several times. There were knife fights and killings just across the street. One night, a man tried to break in while we were there. Peggy and I ran outside to a policeman named "Red", and he told us we should not be living here by ourselves. Until we moved, Red always made a point to check in on us to make sure we were alright.

A friend from the telephone company, Nina, began rooming with Peggy and I. We were always together, every place we went. We enjoyed going to local night clubs as often as we could. The clubs were fun and exciting, and we wanted to drive away every memory we had of that horrible orphanage that had been our home.

One night, the three of us were at a club and we met three men. After the club closed, the men followed us to our apartment. Everyone had been drinking, and as soon as we shut our door, my "date" cornered me in my bedroom. My first sexual encounter was a date rape. I never knew his name. He was a cowboy, and he left his boots on.

The next morning, I was afraid to ask my two girlfriends if they had experienced the same fate. None of us said anything.

Peggy and I enjoyed our time together, but I was much different than she was. I was wild and crazy. And Peggy was much more stable. She ended up getting married and having a wonderful family.

I missed my best friend Peggy, but I quickly found a new one... Peggy's little sister, Marsha Dianne Brady. Since people were always making comments about Marsha Brady on the Brady Bunch, she went by "Dianne". Dianne was a couple years younger than Peggy and I, and she was a big fan of American Bandstand with Dick Clark. She would watch the show each week, and then come over and try to teach me the latest dances. For a fat girl, I had some surprisingly good moves.

People always ask me if Lulu is my real name. No, it's not. Remember Bertha? But I became Lulu when I was 18 years old. I found her in, of all places... jail. I had been arrested for using stolen credit cards.

Some of my friends had asked me if I wanted to go shopping. They didn't tell me that we were going to pay for everything with some credit cards they had stolen. We went to JC Penney, where we bought nice sheets and bedding, cookware, all kinds of stuff. Then my friend said that he wanted to buy a shotgun. He handed me a credit card, and I naively gave it to the cashier. The woman ran the credit card, and then whispered to me, "This card is not yours."

I said, "No, it's my friend's." I turned to point at him, and he was gone.

A few minutes later, I was in handcuffs, headed to the Dallas County jail. They put me in a cell with a couple women who had killed their husbands and with a couple others who were drug dealers. As I looked around, I thought, "I never knew I had it so good back at that orphan's home."

At night, the women would wail and cry. They would cry all night long, and it made me crazy. So, to get them to stop crying, and also to make myself feel better, I would put my hair up in pigtails and start singing and dancing around our cell. I noticed that the crazier and funnier I acted, the better everyone felt. They started laughing instead of crying.

There was an Indian woman in there who had murdered her husband. She had stabbed him to death. She came up to me and said, "You're funny. You make me think of Little Lulu in the comic books. I'm gonna to call you Lulu."

I said, "You can call me anything you want, just keep your hands off me."

I got the name "Lulu" in jail. Named by an Indian woman who had stabbed her husband to death.

My stay in jail ended after one week, thanks to one of my friends who happened to be a prostitute. Cheryl's regular customers included doctors and lawyers, so she asked one of the lawyers to help me. He came down, agreed to represent me, and got me out.

So now you know where Lulu came from. But the story of how I got the name "Roman" is even crazier. After I had lost my job with the phone company, one of my girlfriends said she had an easy way for me to make some money.

My friend knew some very wealthy Filipino men, who had money, but wanted green cards so that they could stay in the U.S. My friend explained to me that the men would pay any woman $1,500 to marry them! Six months later, after they had gotten their green card to become a citizen, they would then divorce the woman, and she could keep the $1,500. I didn't jump at the offer, but another girlfriend did, and she ended up falling in love with her husband, and they stayed married.

As luck would have it, her husband had a friend who was also looking for a "wife", and that's how I met Jose Pizarro Roman.

My girlfriend said, "Joey wants to know if you'll marry him."

I yelled, "No! No way!" and she responded with, "He'll pay you $1,500."

$1,500 was like a million dollars to me at the time. I was fresh out of an orphan's home, and I was dumb as a rock. They explained it all to me, and assured me that I could leave him after six months, once his green card came in. I went for it! And that's how I became Lulu Roman!

We knew that the Immigration and Naturalization Service was not dumb, and they were onto the scheme. So I had to spend a little time learning who "my husband" was. I had to learn what he liked, what his favorite foods were, what movies he liked... I spent three or four months getting to know all about him. And luckily I did, because the INS asked me lots of questions, trying to make sure that we were really in love.

We got married at the Justice of the Peace in downtown Dallas. When we walked out onto the curb, I turned to my new husband and I said, "Give me my money."

But he just smiled and said, "Oh no. You my wife. You go home with me."

I yelled, "Give me my money!"

Again, he said, "No. You my wife. You go home with me."

I told him, in no uncertain terms, that I would not be going home with him. I ended up hailing a cab and left him standing at the curb. There was no honeymoon.

When he refused to give me my money, I had the marriage annulled, and then I had Jose deported! He was sent back to the Philippine Islands. After I made it big on Hee Haw, I imagined Jose sitting in his hut in the Philippines, watching a little black and white TV, yelling, "That my wife! That my wife!"

Now, all these years later, with Hee Haw still airing in reruns, he's probably a tiny, old man, still in the Philippines, watching TV and whispering, "That my wife." Yes, I got rid of my husband, but I decided to keep his name of Roman.

SEX, DRUGS AND… MORE SEX

I could have used the $1,500 that Jose had promised me to support my fast-growing drug habit. I was already a drug addict by the time I left the orphan's home. Almost from the very moment I stepped out into "the real world", I just went crazy. I completely wasted the next decade of my life with drugs. I felt so ugly and so unwanted, and getting high was my way of forgetting that for a few minutes.

Like most druggies, I started out smoking marijuana. Of course, this was the 1960s, and I was a true hippie. Everyone smoked weed back then. But I could smoke anybody under the table. I smoked so much of it that even my dog got high! I had a little puppy who liked to sit on my lap. When I smoked and got high, he also felt the effect, and he really started to like it. Any time I got out a doobie, he would jump up in my lap. I named him Stoney.

My friend Dianne and I did a lot of drugs together. We were like Laverne and Shirley… if Laverne and Shirley had been on drugs. We were stoned out of our minds most of the time.

I threw a birthday party for her, and I made marijuana brownies. Dianne was sitting in a big bean bag chair when she laid down her plate of brownies, and my dog ate them. That dog got so stoned. We had a poster of Jimmy Hendrix on the wall, and that dog just sat and stared at that poster. My friends who came over for the party all laughed about it…But soon, my drug habit was no laughing matter. I quickly progressed way past smoking marijuana to dropping LSD. When I took my first LSD pill, I loved it. I saw colors I didn't know existed. I never saw pink elephants or anything, but it played tricks on my mind. I got to a point where I could take twenty-five hits of it at one time. I was so big, I had a big tolerance level. Whatever it was, I could do more than anybody else. I probably shouldn't say this, but for some reason, I never had a bad trip. It was always great... until I came down.

Then things really got bad. I started shooting up. After I'd worn out the veins in my arm, I started putting the needles in all over my body. I used to have an "X" in between my fingers. I would pump up my fist so that I could see the veins, and I would shoot up my drugs on that "X". I would mainline speed into my hand. If I couldn't hit the vein, I would try to shoot up in the back of my leg. On the rare occasion that that didn't work, I had a friend up shoot me up in the jugular vein of my neck. I only did that a couple times, because it was very scary. You wanted to make sure your friend could hit that vein dead-on, or you could end up dead. Of course, if you hit the vein just right, you could also end up dead from the drugs you were putting into it.

To pay for my drugs, my friend Carol offered an interesting suggestion. Carol and I were sharing an apartment. I knew she didn't have a job, but she would always easily come up with her portion of the rent. When I asked her what her secret was, she confided to me that she had a "sugar daddy". She explained that a sugar daddy was a rich guy who would give you money, expensive gifts, and basically anything else you needed or wanted... as long as you were always there to show him a good time. Carol also admitted that she had a number of different sugar daddies.

One of those was a man who was part of the Neiman Marcus company. Not only did he work there, but he was also one of the very rich family members! Carol always joked that he worked for "Needless Markup". Carol took him for so much money. Of course, she earned it too. He was such a fan of hers that he gave her a 1965 powder blue Ford Mustang.

With Carol showing me the way, I found my own sugar daddies. I also found out that most of the men were not only rich and powerful, but many were religious leaders! One of mine was the head of Bible Schools for the Dallas Independent School District. But that was nothing, compared to the man who was in charge of the financial bookkeeping for a well-known crusade!

That man wanted to be a sugar daddy to both Carol and I! And we showed him a great time. He would sling money at us. It was all great fun… until his wife came after us with a gun! She actually chased us all the way to my great grandmother's house. We pounded on that door, and Granny let us in just before the woman caught up to us.

As we struggled to catch our breath inside, the woman was out on the step, yelling, "I'm gonna kill her! She slept with my husband!"

Granny was in her nightgown. She didn't have her hearing aids in, and she was yelling, "What's going on?!"

Claudine was also there, and she grabbed her shotgun and started cussing at the man's wife. Carol was so scared she peed all over the floor!

Finally, the police came and took the woman away. The following week, she got Grandma Imogene's phone number and called her. Granny was so upset with me, and I'm sure our sugar daddy couldn't wait for the next crusade to start so that he could hit the road.

When the policemen responded to our call, I recognized a couple of the officers. I had become friends with them through a girlfriend I'd made at the telephone company. Her name was Sissy, and she loved cops. She loved showing her "support" to the men in blue… sometimes right in their patrol car!

I learned most of my lovemaking techniques from Sissy, and in no time, I became a sex machine. I found that sex gave me self-esteem. The more sex I had, the more I thought I was being loved and accepted. All those years spent in the orphan's home, with no one ever holding or hugging me, and no one ever telling me that they loved me, had taken a huge toll. Now, any time a man wanted to touch me, for whatever reason, I was going to jump at the chance!

I gave myself to many men, trying to make myself believe that I was loveable. On some nights I had one man, but on many others, I'd have two or even three. I'd make a date with one at 7:00, then I'd meet another guy at 9:00, and then another at 11:00. After being told for my entire life that no one would ever want me because I was fat, I was pleasantly surprised to find that many men were attracted to large women.

My partners included lawyers, doctors, bartenders, carpenters, teachers, shoe salesmen, rock stars, soldiers, CPAs, dentists, and many whom I never bothered to find out what they did for a living. I became a great lover. I learned little tricks to do with my mouth and my body, and I could satisfy any man I was with.

I had no regard for my body or my health. All I thought about was getting all the sex I could. I thought that that made me acceptable. If a man was having sex with me, then they must like me. After being told all my life that I was fat, ugly, and worthless, it felt good to turn a man on.

That's how I lived my life for many years. Sex and drugs. That's all I lived for. But I knew, if I kept it up, I wouldn't be living much longer. I didn't care. If this was all life had to offer, then if I died, I wouldn't be missing much.

At that point in my life, I was so miserable I didn't care about anything. In the 60s, we were into free love. But I found out that free love was very costly. I was also into the numerology stuff too. I was just a miserable soul. I did more drugs than anybody I've ever known. I'm sure there are many people out there who did more drugs than I did, but I never met them, and most of them are probably dead. I had a number of friends who died because they couldn't stop doing drugs. I should have been dead many, many times.

If you have no concept of what love is to any degree, then you have no fear, because you have nothing to lose. That's the way I lived. People would never dream that I have done the stuff that I've done. I did everything I could to destroy myself. But God never let it happen. God protected me through all those crazy years. He had much bigger plans for me.

At the time, I had no aspirations at all. I had no dreams for any kind of life. I didn't allow myself to dream. As I was trying to stick a needle full of drugs into my arm, if I could have seen the future that God had coming for me, I would have thought I was on the biggest drug trip ever! That would have been much more impressive than any flying pink elephant!

THE BIGGEST GO-GO DANCER IN DALLAS, TEXAS

Could God's grand plan for me have included a go-go club in Dallas? I guess I will have to ask God that one when I get to Heaven. But for now, that looks entirely possible.

Thanks to angry wives with guns, Carol and I saw our sugar daddy riches get cut off. So, Carol decided that she now wanted to try her hand at a "more honest" profession. She wanted to be an exotic dancer!

She asked if I would go along with her, to check out one of the nightclubs in downtown Dallas. The club had been owned by Jack Ruby. Jack was the man who shot and killed Lee Harvey Oswald on live TV after the death of President Kennedy. Jack was in partnership with people who owned the Theater Lounge and the Colony Club.

The best dancer those clubs had was a girl who was billed as "Chris Colt, the Girl with the 45s". She had a big, gold pointed bra, and it was full! This was long before implants, and she was 100% real. During our visit, the club manager told Carol that she should come back on amateur night. That would be the perfect time for her to show off her "talent". And a few nights later, that's exactly what she did. As soon as she got up on stage, everyone in the place could see that she was one hot little gal. They loved her.

But all the other amateur night dancers were horrible. As I watched them from the audience, I said very loudly, "Lord a mercy, I could do better than that!"

And this old guy with a smoker's voice replied, "I bet you fifty bucks you can't."

I turned around to him and said, "I bet you fifty bucks I can!"

The man's name was Pappy Dolsen. He smoked big cigars. Pappy was the man who booked every woman who danced in all the strip joints in Dallas, and he said to me, "You got one week to get ready." Pappy hired Carol that night, and she went by the name Jade East. She was very pretty and sexy, and she got quite popular.

I knew there was no way I could be sexy like Carol. I weighed 300 pounds! So I came up with the idea of acting silly. When I got up on stage, I made funny faces and did funny poses, as I "stripped" down to a bra and bloomers. And I won the amateur night hands down! Pappy not only lost his fifty dollar bet to me, but he hired me to start dancing in his clubs. He agreed to pay me a dollar a pound! That first week, I made $300.

My stage name was "Little Lulu". I wore breakaway clothes, and I could make just one quick pull and my entire outfit would fall off. I put a little padlock over my private area. The drunks would yell, "You got a key for that thing baby?!" and I'd respond right back, "You have to blow it off!"

I was a comedian, and not a real stripper, but I danced in the Spot 77 and The Busy Bee. I danced in three or four clubs each week.

The Spot 77 club was located next to the Dewey Grooms Longhorn Ballroom. Lots of country music stars played at the Ballroom, including Conway Twitty, Tammy Wynette, Charley Pride, and Loretta Lynn.

I was picking up my paycheck one night, when a friend of mine, Jimmy Velvet, stopped us in the parking lot. Jimmy sang like Frank Sinatra, and he had been friends with Elvis. Jimmy said, "Guess who is playing in the Ballroom... Buck Owens!" Carol loved Buck Owens, and she was so excited. Of course, I was a hippie go-go dancer and not a country music fan, so I had no idea who Buck Owens was. But that was about to change!

Jimmy Velvet took us backstage to meet Buck, and when Buck saw Carol, he fell in love. For a couple years after that, any time Buck got close to Dallas, he would come to see Carol. And while Carol was with Buck, I was having a fling with his guitar player Don Rich. Since Carol and I were always together, Buck and I got to know each other, and we became good friends.

Buck told me, "Lulu, you are one of the funniest people I've ever met. One of these days, you are gonna be a big star… and I'm going to have something to do with it."

I flicked his cowboy hat with my finger and said, "Keep talkin', baby!"

I really didn't think anything about Buck's off-the-cuff promise. I just figured he was a big cowboy, country singer, who talked that way to every fat girl he liked. But I soon learned to never doubt Buck Owens.

HELLO HEE HAW

Since I was making it big in the strip joints, I thought I'd act like I was rich, and I had a phone put in next to my bathtub. To me, that was the ultimate in high class! And I just happened to be taking a bath when my new phone rang. It was the call that changed my entire life.

"Lulu! It's Buck!"

I said, "Buck, are you in town? I'm here in my tub just waiting on you!"

Buck laughed and said back, "No, I'm not in town. But do you remember when I told you I was going to have a hand in making you a star?"

My mind was already turning, as I said: "Yes, I do."

"Well, this is it," Buck said. "I want you to be on a TV show with me called Hee Haw."

"He-what?!" I asked.

Buck laughed, "Hee Haw! Like a donkey! It's a country music version of 'Laugh-In', and they want you to play Goldie Hawn's part."

I yelled into the phone, "Goldie Hawn?! She's that skinny blonde!"

Buck paused and laughed, "Well, they want you to kind of be the opposite of Goldie Hawn. You need to call American Airlines, and they'll have a first class ticket to Hollywood waiting for you."

Here's a little background on how the Hee Haw show started: in 1968, one of the most popular shows on TV was Rowan and Martin's Laugh-In. It featured a large cast, with lots of very fast paced jokes, just one short clip after another. The show aired on NBC, and it seemed like everyone in the country was watching Laugh-In.

Apparently, at least a couple people outside the country were also tuned in. Frank Peppiatt and John Aylesworth, two men who lived in Canada, formed a company that they called Yongestreet Productions. Yonge Street was a main road which ran through their hometown of Toronto. And when John and Frank saw Laugh-In, they came up with the idea of doing a very similar, but very country, version of the show.

Frank and John had worked together on the Jimmy Dean and Andy Williams shows, and were also big fans of country music. When they received the go-ahead from the CBS network to begin putting together a show, instead of doing a cattle call audition for their entire cast, they decided to hire a couple big country music stars and then go from there.

So they went to Las Vegas and hired Roy Clark. Roy was just getting hot, both as an instrumentalist and as a comedian. He was an all-around entertainer. Then Frank and John went to Bakersfield, California and signed Buck Owens. Buck was just about the hottest thing in country music at that time. From 1963 to 1967, every song he released went to number one! He had more than 20 hit songs before he ever started on Hee Haw!

As they visited, John and Frank told Buck that they were looking for a cast that included one gorgeous blonde, one gorgeous brunette, one boy next door type, one girl next door type, one fat, dumb man, and one fat, dumb woman. Buck yelled, "I've got your girl! She's in Dallas."

They must have trusted ol' Buck. They just took his word that the right girl was in Dallas, Texas... and her name was Lulu. I didn't have any acting experience, I knew nothing about country music, and I looked like a 300 pound hippie! But for some reason, Buck had seen something in me. He was one of the few people in my life that ever had faith in me, and his faith helped to change my life.

The next thing I knew, I was on an airplane to Los Angeles. There were no smoking restrictions on planes back then, so I spent most of the flight over in the bathroom, smoking marijuana. Remember, I was still into drugs very heavily, and by the time the plane landed, I was really flying! I'm sure that everyone who went into that bathroom after I came out also got a little high.

I was met at the airport by Buck Owens and a couple of the show producers. They took me to CBS Studios, and the first person I saw there was Carol Burnette. The moment I saw her, my jaw dropped! I was totally speechless. Carol looked at me and said, "Shut your mouth child, you're fixin' to be one of us!"

They took us into Carol's studio, and there was Harvey Korman, Tim Conway and Vicki Lawrence. Their show was on CBS as well, and it was even hotter than Laugh-In.

Since I was so large, I had a tough time finding clothes that fit. So I used my sewing talent I'd learned at the orphanage to make my outfits out of Indian bedspreads! I made two pantsuits, and they had bell bottom sleeves and pants. They were very bright and colorful, and I had my long black hair pulled into pigtails. Tim Conway looked at me and shouted, "Would you look there! There's a real live hippie!"

I could tell some of the TV executives were very puzzled as they stared at me. I saw all these people in the room looking at me with an expression that said, "What are we going to do with that?!"

They were trying to figure out what they were going to put on me for a costume!

Then a man came running toward me, carrying a huge box, and he opened it to show me this great, big, pink dress. They told me to try it on. I did, and it fit me perfectly. Then they told me it was a dress that Jonathan Winters used to wear on his show! One of his most popular characters was an old woman named Maude Frickert. Oh yeah, Jonathan weighed a couple hundred pounds... and when I put on his dress, it looked like it had been tailored just for me!

They asked me to stand in front of a TV camera and read some lines off of a cue card. After I read them, I made a silly face, and everyone in the studio laughed and laughed. I heard one of the producers say to another, "My God, she is incredible!"

I turned to them and said, "Give me your money... and watch me get better."

Years later, Sam Lovullo called me into his office and told me, "There are two people in this cast who we never have to worry about reading their lines. One is Roy Clark, and the other is Lulu Roman. You are the best I've ever seen."

I never thought for a second that I would ever be a TV star. Not when I was a little girl. Not when I was a teenager. It never entered my mind... until I heard the reaction I got from reading that cue card.

During that time, I met the man they planned to play opposite me. They had hired Pat McCormick, who stood 6 feet, 7 inches tall. Later on, he played Big Enos in "Smokey and the Bandit". In that movie, he stood next to the 5 foot, 2 inches Paul Williams... but on Hee Haw, Pat was going to be the fat man, and of course, I was the fat girl.

Back then, there was a popular Clairol hair commercial that showed a couple running through a park in slow motion. In the ad, the woman leaps into the arms of a handsome man. For the Hee Haw pilot, they had me run toward Pat McCormick, and instead of me jumping into his arms, we bumped bellies and fell down.

After my whirlwind trip to Hollywood, I went back to Dallas and waited. For luck, I went to Centennial Park and bought a 24 karat gold toe ring. I still wear it today, and fifty years later, it still fits! I never take it off. Gwen, who went on to be one of the hairdressers at Hee Haw, was with me in the park, and she got a toe ring at the same time that I did. She wore hers for 20 years. But I have never taken mine off! I've worn it through surgeries and everything.

A short time later, I got a letter that said I should be in Nashville for the taping of the show pilot. When I got there, I expected to be working with Pat McCormick, but he was nowhere around. When I asked where Pat was, I was told that he was scared to fly. So he had taken a train from Los Angeles to Nashville. Pat might not have liked flying, but he loved drinking, and he drank almost nonstop during his cross-country train trip. He ended up getting so drunk that, when the train arrived in Nashville, he never got off! He stayed on and took it back to California.

During that time, the producers of Hee Haw decided to replace Pat... ironically, with another man who loved his alcohol. He was a fella named Junior.

Probably the one person I get asked about more than anyone else is Junior Samples. People always want to know if he was acting, or was he really that dumb! I have to tell you that, with Junior, what you saw is what he was. There was no acting whatsoever! I have to admit that when I first met Junior, I couldn't believe he was real. But he was. He was pure in everything he did... and he was pure fun.

Junior lived in Cumming, Georgia, and he loved to fish. One day he caught a big one, and the local radio station did an interview with him about the fish he'd caught. Junior was so funny during that interview that the radio station continued playing it over and over. And then other stations started running it! They ended up making a little 45 rpm record out of the interview. It was just Junior talking, telling the story of "The World's Biggest Whopper." He was just being himself. He didn't even know a tape was running.

Archie Campbell is the person who found Junior Samples for Hee Haw. Archie had already been hired to be on the show, and when he heard Junior talking on the radio, he went to Sam Lovullo, the producer and casting director for the show, and told him he should get him on Hee Haw.

So Sam sent Archie in a big black limousine to Cumming, Georgia. As he drove through town, he happened to see Junior walking down the street. Like always, he was carrying a cane pole and a fishing pail, and he was wearing his overalls. Archie rolled down the limo window and asked, "Hey Junior, do you want to be on TV?"

And Junior said, "Well... I reckon.'"

Junior loved to fish. He also loved to drink. He had a drinking problem. And he had another problem... he stank! When he walked into the studio, everyone took two steps back because he smelled so bad!

But when they put him in front of the camera and asked him to read a cue card, we found out that he had an even bigger problem... Junior could not read. He also couldn't write. He would make an "X" for his signature. So they ended up having someone stand off to the side, say the line, and then Junior would try to repeat what they said.

But when Junior started making some money, he hired someone to teach him how to read and write. When he'd learned to read a little, the guys who wrote the show started trying to find all the words they could that had seven or eight syllables in them, because they knew it would trip Junior up. The most memorable one was the word "trigonometry". They did more than 40 takes, and Junior never could get it right! They finally put Roy Clark in with him, and Roy would say "Trig," and Junior said "Trig."

Roy would say "Oh," and Junior repeated "Oh," and they went through every syllable… and then when Roy said the entire word, Junior shouted, "Tigatomitee!"

When Hee Haw first aired in 1969, it was only supposed to be a summer replacement for the popular Smothers Brothers Show. Of course, the summer of '69 has been going for the last 50 years, because reruns of the show are still airing on TV today!

When Hee Haw started, it had a cast of only about ten people. When it ended its run, there were more than fifty people in the cast. But of the original cast, I am the only one left. As I was writing my book, on November 15, 2018, Roy Clark passed away. I can't believe everyone from our first season is now gone, except for me. It is a lonely feeling. You also can't help having the feeling of "Guess who's next."

Sam Lovullo originally wanted everyone who was on the show each week to sing solos. I told him that I couldn't sing, but he insisted. So they put me in the studio, and I sang "The Only Mama That Will Walk the Line". It was a female version of a big hit for Waylon Jennings. But I sang it so bad, they never aired it! They never showed it to anyone.

I never once thought that I would be a singer. It never entered my head. Little did I know the true miracle that God had waiting for me. But before the fat lady sings… she is going to have to go through hell… as you are about to find out.

Bertha Louise Hable 1947

With Claudine Hable, 1947

The first of many tears to come

18 months old

With my cousins Kathy and Bobby. I'm on the left

*Easter Sunday
at 3 years old*

*A shy Little Red
Riding Hood*

April 1951

*No one wanted to
adopt this sweet
little girl*

*In front of
Harden Hall, 1951*

May 1953

Already getting laughs in 1954

A Junior High Class Photo. I'm in the first row on the far right.

15 years old

A rare peaceful moment with Claudine

School Picture, 1962

March 23, 1963 in a school musical with Zach Ward

School Musical
Kiss Me Kate, 1964

Taking a bow after hearing my first applause

Junior High Graduation

Jan. 1964

Photo booth fun with a classmate Jack Homesley

Finding out that blondes have more fun! With Jack Homesley

With classmate Elaine Gerfolus

My future was so bright, I had to wear shades...to bed!

With John, the man who would father my first child

Painted nails to match my dress. The guy next to me was not impressed!

A true 60s hippie

Wearing rose colored glasses

Partying with Ronnie Hodges from the group The Boxtops

No cell phones in the 60s!

A Polaroid...long before selfies!

Modeling my break-a-way striptease outfit

60s Glamour

*Always the life of
the party*

*In Gatlinburg with
Damon's father John*

Meeting the great Tex Ritter

*Tex was one of the first country
stars I ever met*

With my dear friend Cheryl

With Kris Kristofferson and Rita Coolidge at the Texas International Rock Festival

LU LU
ROMAN

Performers Management
403 Chester Avenue
Bakersfield, Calif. 93301
(805) 323-1101

My first Hee Haw Promo Photo

Hee Haw Cast, Nov. 1969

With that dress, I'm glad they put me in the back!

Hee Haw! 1969

Junior Samples didn't know what to make of Lulu Roman!

But it didn't take him long to warm up to me!

In the haystack with Junior

Behind the Scenes with Junior, 1970

Hippee Lulu with Tammy Wynette

My name in lights...on the Holiday Inn marquee!

With Gordie Tapp

The Hee Haw cast, June 1969.

Baby shower before I had Damon

Most of my friends were girls I danced with in the clubs

With baby Damon, Dec. 1972

In court after my March 18, 1971 arrest. Courtesy AP Wirephoto

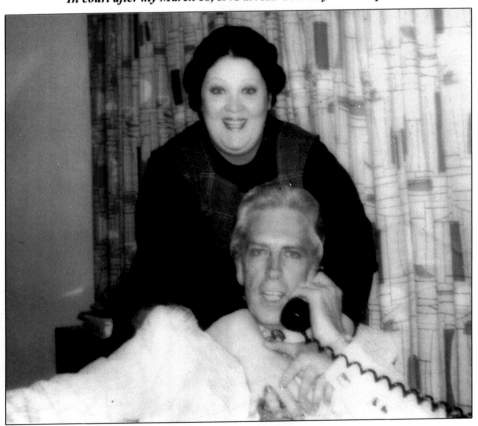

The man who brought me to the Lord, Brother Howard Conatser

Singing in a church, Oct. 1977

On the Hee Haw set, singing my gospel music

I wish I had a dollar for each time I had my bottom swatted by the fence

Never a dull moment with Junior

I still have my waitress uniform from the Truckstop skit

With Archie Campbell,
Gailard Sartain in the
Truckstop

Looking over our lines before shooting a skit

With Damon,
18 months old

Damon visits me on the set

Within the image: *Hotel Fremont Las Vegas Nevada*

Hee Haw comes to Las Vegas

It was a big day when Big Bird visited the Kornfield

Junior always wearing his overalls, even backstage at the Opry

I loved Roy Rogers and Dale Evans

The cast runs through a later appearance of Roy and Dale

In the cornfield with Slim Pickens

Elizabeth Linneman touches up Buck's makeup.

A Valentine photo shoot with Buck Owens

Never ask if Buck Owens was a good sport. He was!

Waiting on Doc Campbell

The doctor will see you now.

My son Justin, 1 year old

Singing with the great Roy Acuff, June 1989

Mr. Acuff was still handsome, even in overalls

Behind the scenes on the Gossipy set

Now we're not ones to go 'round spreadin' rumors...

Behind the scenes on the Culhanes set

The Culhane Family

The Culhanes. They put me next to Grandpa to make me look even bigger!

I'm ready for my closeup!

Cracking up the legendary Barbara Mandrell

I loved Grandpa Jones!

Marty Robbins and Barbara Mandrell joined us to play in the All American Country Games

Linda Thompson, me, Misty Rowe, doing our best Charlie's Angels pose!

REAL LIFE IS NO KORNFIELD KOUNTY

I lived in Dallas the entire time that we filmed Hee Haw. I had always lived in Texas. Texas was big, and so resilient. Texas was always the biggest, baddest, and greatest place to live and play. I just loved it.

For many years, Hee Haw was filmed at WTVF in Nashville. We shared the TV studios with the Channel 5 news staff. In 1974, WTVF hired the first black female co-anchor in Nashville. Her name was Oprah Winfrey. I wish we had thought to get Oprah to tape a segment in the cornfield before she moved on to bigger and better things!

But Nashville was not appealing to me for many years. When I first came to Nashville, I thought everyone was a cowboy. I had no idea it would have such a vast amount of talent and such a vast amount of possibilities of things to do. I finally moved to Nashville… the year we stopped doing Hee Haw!

We filmed an entire year's worth of shows in June and October. Those were the only two months we worked on the show, so we had the other ten months of the year to do other things. During the rest of the year, Buck and Roy recorded new songs and went back out on tour, while I went back home to Texas.

So what did I do when I went back home? You have to remember that when I left to be on the show, I had been a 300 pound go-go dancer! A go-go dancer with a growing drug problem. You couldn't tell it when you watched me in the cornfield during the first season or two, but I was still that same hippie druggy who cussed like a sailor. I wasn't into country music. I was into acid rock. You would have found me listening to the Moody Blues, not Merle Haggard.

When I got back to Dallas, I went right back into my unhealthy lifestyle. It was all I knew. But now, I could do my drugs while I watched myself on television! The first Hee Haw shows were so cornball. They were horrible, and if you want to do something wild, you ought to try to watch one of those first shows when you are completely stoned! That's exactly what I did.

On June 15, 1969, I got all of my friends together to watch the debut of Hee Haw. We smoked as much marijuana as we possibly could, as we watched the premiere episode, and we found that the more we smoked, the funnier the show got!

Apparently, the TV critics across the country were not smoking anything, because each and every one of them said that Hee Haw was the worst show they had ever seen!

Some said it had to be the worst show in the history of television! But a funny thing happened… many of those reviews were so negative that people started tuning in to the show, just to see how bad we were!

The critics were unanimous in proclaiming that the show would never last! I wonder what those critics think now, when they turn on RFD TV and Hee Haw re-runs are still on the air?! Even before the continuous re-runs started, Hee Haw had become the longest-running weekly first run syndicated show in the history of television!

I had a cute boyfriend named Randy, and he had a friend named John. They were best friends, and we all hung out and got stoned together. When Randy got word he was being sent to Vietnam, John assured him that he would take care of me.

And he did! I fell in love with him. It wasn't something we had planned on. It just happened. We just fell into it. I was crazy about him, and he was crazy about me. When Randy came back from Vietnam, he was really messed up. He slept with a gun under his pillow, and would wake up screaming in the middle of the night, "Get the gun! Get the gun!"

Then he'd calm down as he kept talking in his sleep, and he'd say, "Lulu will protect me. Lulu will take care of me."

I wanted to protect Randy. But I was in love with his friend John. We had started out as good friends, but the more we got to know each other, the more we fell for each other. I didn't know what love was. I didn't have a concept of love. For a long time, I didn't even know that I was in love with John. But I knew that I really cared about him.

John was tall and thin. He had long, curly blonde hair with a mustache, and he had beautiful lips. He loved my sense of humor, and he had a crazy sense of humor that I loved. We used to run up to the tarmac at Dallas Love Field, and we would lay down on our backs and watch the planes fly right over us as they were landing. I'm sure the pilots were freaking out. We were crazy.

John was from Tennessee, and when I came to Nashville to tape Hee Haw, he came with me. The sun always seemed to be shining in Nashville. As soon as we got back home to Texas, however, things turned very, very dark.

On March 18, 1971, police raided my home in Dallas. They found 250 kilos of marijuana, along with assorted narcotics and some LSD. They took me straight to jail, and when the dust had settled, I was facing four years in prison for possession of dangerous drugs. My attorney appealed the sentence, and that allowed me to stay out of jail for the time being.

Of course, word of my arrest quickly made it to the producers of Hee Haw. A lot has changed since 1971, but back then, Lulu Roman was one of the very first TV stars to be arrested for a serious offense. If I had gone to jail, it would have been a horrible thing for the show and for the sponsors. I was let go from Hee Haw.

They didn't really fire me, but they kind of eased me out of the show. I was immediately taken out of the opening credits. When it came time to tape the next year's worth of shows, I noticed my phone never rang to tell me when to come to Nashville. I was heartbroken.

So what do you think I did? I started doing even more drugs. At first, I was using drugs just to get high. But then I started taking them to try to go away... permanently. I tried to commit suicide a couple times. I would take a handful of pills and go to sleep. But I always, somehow, managed to wake up the next morning.

On one occasion though, I came especially close to not waking up. I had taken 30 Valiums, along with 20 other pills. When my friend Cheryl found me, she couldn't bring me around. She was heavily into speed at the time, so she thought a shot of speed would help balance out all the downers I had taken.

It worked. I did wake up.

Cheryl and I always joked that we wouldn't live to reach thirty years old. Unfortunately, that prediction came true for one of us.

It was during this glorious (said sarcastically) time in my life that I found out I was pregnant! Luckily, I did know who the father was. Even though John and I had never married, we were both in love with each other. Our friendship was such a bond. I had never wanted to have any children until I met John. Now, even with my life being such a wreck, I wanted to have his baby. And I did.

But the big happy family I had dreamed of never came true. I know that John loved me, but he was not a one-woman man. We had a lot of ups and downs together in our relationship. John would go to the bars, meet a pretty girl and take off with her. Yes, things like that were a little hard on a relationship!

We were having one of those down times when I found out I was pregnant. I had to track John down at one of his hangouts, and when he saw my quickly growing stomach, he put his hand on my tummy and said, "That ain't my kid."

I said, "F you! It is your kid! But don't you ever come around and try to lay claim to this baby."

I was alone. I was out of work and destitute. And now I was pregnant. When word of my pregnancy reached the Hee Haw set, I received a call from Sam Lovullo. He was the producer, and really, the man in charge of the entire show. But Sam was also like a daddy to me, and also to everyone else on the show. He was like an Italian Godfather. He just took care of everybody.

Sam wasn't calling to offer me my job back, but he wanted me to know that I was never officially fired. He told me that he'd considered it a little break. A short time later, I opened my mailbox to find a check from Sam's personal account.

He sent me money every month that I was off the show. He took care of me, and nobody knew he was helping me. Sam Lovullo was the best man in the world.

My best friend at the time, Cheryl, took me to the hospital when I went into labor. She dropped me off and then went back to our apartment, and while she was there… somebody stole my car. Yes, there would be nothing routine about the birth of Lulu Roman's first child!

On November 15, 1972, it snowed in Dallas, Texas. I had been watching the snow fall as I went into labor. But the peaceful scene outside was just the opposite of what was about the happen inside that hospital delivery room.

My body was not made to have children. I had big pelvis bones that would not move. I should have had a regular Cesarean section birth, but they waited too long for it. The doctor just butchered me. He did such a horrible job that I had to go back and have an operation for them to repair all the damage they had done to me.

That was awful enough, but my baby had an even bigger problem. When a mother-to-be is a drug addict, every drug she takes also gets into the body of her unborn child. And I had done drugs throughout every month of my pregnancy. Can you believe that not one person ever came to me and said, "You really shouldn't be shooting up when you're pregnant"? But I'd had no one who cared at all about me or about my baby.

When my baby boy was born, he was addicted to drugs. He wasn't breathing when the doctor picked him up. Once they were able to get some breath into his lungs, they put him in an incubator and rushed him across town to the Children's Medical Center. On their way out of the room, I heard the doctor tell the nurse, "He won't make it."

The doctors told me that my baby had infant respiratory distress syndrome. While it was caused by my drug use, that same disease had killed the newborn baby of President Kennedy nine years earlier. Even with the greatest care, and all the money in the world, the President's baby Patrick had only lived two days.

My son was born with fluid in his lungs because of the amphetamines I had been taking each day when I was pregnant. I wanted to go with my baby, but I couldn't, because I was fighting for my own life after the doctor had cut me so bad. So I lay in the bed, crying as I thought of my poor little boy in an ambulance speeding across Dallas. It was then that I said the first real prayer of my life.

At that time, I had no relationship at all with God. If I believed in him at all, I hated him, because he had never given me a mom or dad who loved me. But when they told me my baby was not going to live through the night, I reached out to God. But my prayer didn't start with "Dear God..." Instead, I said, "Yo Dude..."

I was still a hippie, so it was a hippie prayer. I'm sure it wasn't a proper prayer. But I was as sincere as I could possibly be. I begged God to save the life of my child. I said, "God, if you are there, if you will let my baby live, I will change my ways. I will stop doing drugs. I will try to be the person you want me to be. I will live my life for you."

The first time I touched my child, he was already ten days old. I was released from the hospital just before Thanksgiving Weekend, but my baby was still being treated at the Children's Medical Hospital. On Black Friday, the day after Thanksgiving, a nurse called me and said, "You had better get over here right away. There has been a change in your baby's condition."

When I ran into the hospital, a doctor met me and said, "Miss Roman, I really don't know what to say to you. Most of the regular doctors are off for the holiday, but they had told me your baby was dying. But I just cannot find anything wrong with him."

Other doctors came in and checked my baby all over, and they couldn't find anything wrong with him either! He was breathing normally on his own. They wrote on his medical records, "Act of God". I have no doubt that the Lord touched that baby and healed him. I picked up my child and took him home. I had a lot to be thankful for that Thanksgiving.

God had heard my hippie prayer, and God had saved my baby's life. God was true to his word. But I was not true to mine. I went another six months doing the same horrible things I had been doing. I continued using drugs, and I went right back to selling dope to help pay for my rent and food. Little did I know, though, that by next Thanksgiving, Lulu Roman would be a completely different person.

I named my baby Damon Erik. A week after he came home, my phone rang. Of course it was John, and he whispered, "Can I see my boy?"

"You S.O.B., of course you can," I said. I never had a daddy, and I wanted my child to have a father. John came over and ended up staying a few months. But then he ran off again, and I wouldn't see him again until Damon was eleven years old.

For the longest time, I didn't want to have kids. I was afraid to, because I had no idea how to take care of a child. I had no one to teach me. I had no mother of my own to teach me anything.

My friend Cheryl is the one who taught me how to take care of Damon. Cheryl had three kids, and she knew it all. She was smart and classy. She was wild and reckless, uninhibited and fun. She was also a prostitute, and one of her customers was a doctor… the same doctor who ended up delivering my baby! Small world.

Damon was a beautiful baby. He had light brown hair with hazel green eyes. People would come up to me and say, "Your baby is just gorgeous. What's her name?"

I'd reply, "Her name is Damon. She's a boy!"

When Damon was ten years old, he was diagnosed with Tourette syndrome. He would jerk his head, and kind of bark. He had outbursts and muscle ticks. When we found out he had it, I prayed and prayed that he would not have the kind where you scream out curse words. I praise God that his Tourette's is very mild.

Damon was like me: he was the underdog. He was one everyone made fun of. They made fun of him because of his Tourette's. But if it bothered him, he really kept it to himself. He didn't let anyone see if it upset him.

I am very proud of the man Damon grew up to be. For quite some time, he worked with special needs children in the Seattle school system, and he was so awesome with them. He had a great way of handling kids who had anger issues. They would often get violent, but he was always able to get them to calm down.

Damon also worked in a bank, during his time in Washington. But in the Fall of 2018, he moved back to Nashville to be near his dear ol' mom. I was so happy when he told me he was moving back. One of the proudest moments of my life was when Damon told me, "Mom, I am so glad that God let you be my mother." And the thing I am most thankful for is that Damon loves the Lord with all his heart.

FROM JAIL TO JESUS

Only by the grace of God had I been able to stay out of prison after my drug arrest in 1971. As part of my sentence for that arrest, I was given a ten year probation. When you are addicted to drugs, ten years is a mighty long time to go without getting into any trouble. I didn't come close. In 1973, all hell broke loose.

One of the best friends I've ever had is Camille. But everybody calls her "Molly". I met Molly when she was sixteen years old; she had come to babysit for me. Molly and I did a lot of drugs together. We both fought many of the same battles over the years, and we both finally won those battles. It's a true miracle that we both made it through all those crazy times. Today, I can honestly say that Molly has been a lifelong friend.

But in 1973, Molly knew that, when I was not using drugs myself, I was selling them to other people. As much as I hate to say it, I had turned into a drug dealer. I packaged and weighed everything, and then sold it to those who were hooked, just like I was.

On March 28, 1973, Molly was sitting in a car outside my apartment in Dallas. She and a friend were smoking a doobie, when they saw some police coming their way, and right there, Molly and her friend ate that marijuana! They swallowed all they had, and just as the last of it went down their throats, the police passed right by them!

But Molly's relief turned to horror, as she watched the cops getting ready to bust down my apartment door! I grabbed my four month old baby as the police kicked in the door. In their search, the police had no trouble in finding LSD, marijuana, and lots of drug paraphernalia. It was all over my apartment. I was an addict.

As the police arrested me, they also wanted to take my baby... but I saw Molly in the doorway, and I told the police, "This is my babysitter. She will take care of my child."

She took him and ran out. Molly and her parents took care of Damon while I was in jail. I will always be grateful to them for that.

I will also be thankful for the kindness that my grandmother Claudine showed, at that time. For all of her faults – and there were MANY – on this occasion, she did help me. She bailed me out of the Dallas County jail, using the deed to some land that she had. But she was so mad at me.

While my life had literally gone to hell, the life of my old friend Dianne Brady had conversely gone in just the opposite direction. We had lost touch over the years, but during that time, Dianne had found the Lord. She became very religious. She was saved, and became Born Again, and now her old friend Lulu was sitting in jail. Yes, she had gone her way, and I had gone mine.

Dianne later told me that the first time she'd seen me on Hee Haw, she was so shocked. She was stunned! She called her sister Peggy and yelled, "Did you see Lu on TV?!"

A couple years later, I would shock her yet again. She was sitting at her dining room table, with all her friends from church. Those ladies were all so young and innocent. They didn't know anything about her drug past. But one of them was reading the newspaper, and said, "Look at this! Lulu from Hee Haw got busted for drugs!"

Dianne's church friends were shocked, as she quietly said, "I know her. She was a dear friend who was in the orphan's home with me."

Dianne told them, "I have no idea how to get ahold of her."

"Let's just pray that you will be able to find her," her friends said. And they prayed.

Three days later, Dianne was working in a building in downtown Dallas, and as she was getting ready to step off of an elevator, the door opened… and there I stood. I had just gotten out of jail, and I was going up to meet a doctor who always gave me drugs. I never learned! Dianne wanted to talk, but I was in a hurry. I was also embarrassed for her to see me, and to see the horrible person I had turned into. But for some reason, as the elevator door was closing, I yelled my phone number to her.

Events like this show you who your true friends really are. That night, Dianne called me, and said, "I'm coming to see you right now."

When I opened the door for her, instead of saying hello, I asked, "What in the world has happened to you? You look so strange."

"Lulu," Dianne replied, "I found Jesus."

I laughed and said, "I didn't know he was missing!"

But Dianne just smiled back at me, saying, "I met him."

"You met who?" I asked.

"I met God. God got me."

Dianne told me about God, and about how God loved me. When we were teenagers, Dianne had the same horrible, crude language that I did – that I still had! But I could see how God had just cleaned up Dianne's mouth. She didn't talk the same.

A few days later, Dianne came to visit me again, and this time she brought her friend Paula. When I opened my front door, there they both stood, with their arms filled with bags of groceries. They were surrounded by diapers, baby clothes, and a hundred jars of baby food. I was speechless. Nobody had ever done anything like that for me. I didn't know what to say.

I was so thankful for everything. I asked them what I could do in return, and Dianne said, "There is one thing. There's some place I want to take you."

I said, "If it's your church, I am not interested."

"Lou," she whispered, "all they want to do is love you."

I had no desire to go to church, but I felt obligated, since they had brought me all the baby food and clothes. So I told them I would go... one time.

I kept my word to Dianne, but on the day I was going to go with her to church, guess how I got ready... I did my usual shooting up. At that time, I was mainlining drugs. I was shooting needles filled with drugs directly into my veins. To cover up the needle marks in my arm, I made sure to put on a long sleeve blouse. And as we headed off to church, Dianne had no idea that I had shot up with drugs just before the service.

I hadn't been inside a church since I was in the orphanage. Now, I was quite apprehensive, as Dianne and I sat together in the very back of the Beverly Hills Baptist Church in Dallas. But the Spirit of the Lord didn't care where we were sitting. Almost immediately, I became overwhelmed with the Spirit. It touched my heart so much, I couldn't stop crying.

I know that God dropped me in the middle of those people. I didn't realize that they all knew who I was, and that they were all praying for me. I could tell almost instantly that none of these people were "faking their faith." They were real. I turned my attention to the pastor, who was talking up front.

I became mesmerized by Brother Howard Conatser. He was definitely a man of God. He was 6'3", with silver hair and blue eyes that were the color of the sky. He was very smart, and so informed of the Bible. He had an anointing on him like no other I've known.

Then, through my tears, I saw the pastor walking right toward us! He took my hand and introduced me to the congregation. Of course, everyone knew who I was. They knew me from Hee Haw. They also knew me from the drug bust that had been printed on the front of the newspaper.

The women of the church all gathered around me, and they prayed for me. But I was fighting them all the way. Even with my life in shambles, I was still not wanting to give up my destructive ways... but that experience was enough to draw me back to the church the next week.

Again, we sat in a back pew, but I paid much more attention to the service, and then I started noticing everyone around us. They were all speaking in gibberish! Some were praying with others, and then all of a sudden one person would just fall down, completely passed out. At first it was just one or two, and then they all started dropping like flies! I yelled out, "My God, Dianne! These people are all freaking out on acid!"

And Dianne said, "No, they are talking in tongues."

I got a little more used to everyone over the next couple of weeks. During one of the services, I whispered to Dianne that I wanted to talk with Brother Howard. She went running up to him, and he stopped the entire service and sent everyone else home! Then he led us to his office.

Pastor Howard asked me, "Do you want to know Jesus?"

"I think I do," I said.

Brother Howard looked me in the eye, and replied, "First of all, don't you toy with this. This will change your life forever."

I told Pastor Howard, "I am 26 years old. I've had everything this world could offer me. I've gone through men, money, sex, drugs, fame. I've had it all, and I was still so miserable that I got busted for drug possession two times."

We sat on the floor and he took my hands in his, as he explained in very simple terms how Jesus could change my entire world.

As Pastor Howard listened, I came up with every reason in the world not to be saved, including "I'm not giving up my men."

Pastor Howard said, "God will take care of that."

I came back with, "I'm not giving up my drugs."

Again, Pastor Howard calmly stated, "God will take care of that."

Every time I'd say something, he would just say to me, "God will take care of that."

Finally, Pastor Howard asked, "Are you ready?"

"I guess I am," I said.

Pastor Howard was the godliest man I ever knew. Just like everyone else, he was not perfect, but he was the greatest example of unconditional love to me. Outside of my closest friends like Dianne and Peggy, Pastor Howard loved me more than anyone in my life. I was very blessed to have a pastor who was such a man of God, but he was also a very, very dear friend. And the people of that church literally loved the hell out of Lulu Roman.

On April 11, 1973, Pastor Howard had me pray the sinner's prayer, and I asked Jesus to come into my heart and to change me. It was very simple. But as we got up… I started dancing.

It was like every burden had been lifted off of me! I was floating. I had never felt that good when I had been high on drugs.

I was still in a state of joy when Dianne dropped me off at home, and when I woke up the next morning, I immediately got dressed and started cleaning up my house. I thought, if I was going to clean up my life, I might as well start with my apartment!

At around noon that day, I looked at my watch and realized, "Wow, I haven't had any drugs since yesterday." I had been heavily doing meth and speed every day. I knew I was probably due to start having major withdrawals, so I called Dianne and asked her to come over and stay with me.

Dianne helped me finish cleaning my house, and we played some cards and had lunch.

We both kept watching the clock, as we waited for me to get sick from coming off the drugs. We enjoyed some tea, as we waited, and waited, and waited for the withdrawals to kick in. To this day, it has now been almost 50 years, and I am still waiting for a drug craving! It never came! I had been instantly delivered from drugs the moment I gave my heart to the Lord. It just went away. I never had a desire to do drugs ever again.

Neither my body nor my mind went through any kind of withdrawals. The Lord just took it all away. It was an amazing miracle. God delivered me from drugs.

A few months later, on July 7, 1973, I was baptized with the Holy Spirit. It took place during a Saturday evening service, at a tiny, spirit-filled Baptist church in Garland, Texas.

LOST AND FOUND

After I'd gotten saved, one of the first people I called was my dear friend Cheryl. Cheryl was the prostitute who had helped me so much when Damon was born. I told her, "I got saved, and I want to tell you about Jesus."

But Cheryl said, "No. I've got time. I'll hear about it later."

But she didn't have time. In December, 1974, I went to Israel with my church group, and before I got back, Cheryl was dead. On December 15th, they found Cheryl, sitting on the floor in an apartment in Tyler, Texas. One end of a rope was tied around her neck. The other end was strung over the door. The police called it a suicide. They said that she had hanged herself, to which I yelled, "Bull S--t!"

I knew she didn't kill herself.

After the investigation was completed, they determined that Cheryl was murdered over a bad drug deal. Cheryl's youngest son grew up to be a police officer in Dallas. A couple years ago, many decades after her death, her son called me to let me know they had finally found the person who murdered my best friend. A detective going through cold cases in Dallas was able to solve the case.

Many years before, Cheryl had predicted she wouldn't live to be 30. Sadly, that premonition had come true, as she tragically lost her life at the age of 29. It just broke my heart when Cheryl was killed. I just pray that she had one second to call on the name of Jesus. I tried to tell her. You hear people talk about the fires of Hell. That fire is probably pretty painful, but I think there is a far worse punishment, and that would be for the people there to remember all the times that someone offered the salvation to Jesus to them and they said no.

Another soul I worried about was for that of my mother, Clara Gene. After I became born again, I went to her and asked if she knew Jesus. She laughed, "Oh, hell no! My husband's goin' to Hell and I'm goin' with him!"

Over the next few decades, I was able to help bring thousands of people to the Lord... but I could never get through to my own mother. It broke my heart, but people have to make their own decisions.

Even though I had been saved and had completely changed my life, I was still in so much trouble. Thanks to my earlier drug arrest, I was looking at 20 years in the state penitentiary! It was pretty apparent that I was going to end up in the Texas Women's Prison for a long time.

I didn't have a prayer. Oh yes, I did! I had thousands of prayers. They were all being sent up on my behalf each day. I was a member of the Church on the Rock. It had started as the Beverly Hills Baptist Church in Dallas. We'd moved from a little church into a huge bowling alley. That move was needed, as the church congregation had grown from 150 people to 10,000, and all of those people were praying for Lulu Roman!

Every time the phone rang, I expected the worst. I knew it would be someone telling me that my court date was set. I was facing seven or eight felony charges, along with a misdemeanor. I waited and waited, but the authorities never pursued anything! I didn't know why, but no court or jail officials ever contacted me. It had to be a miracle.

Many years later, I found out that there was a spirit-filled little lady who worked at the courthouse. She had hidden some of my court papers in the back of her drawer, so the court officials and police would not come looking for me. She had buried those papers.

For the next year and a half, I devoted myself to serving the Lord. I was out there giving my testimony in every church that would have me. I was a completely changed person. I'll tell you much more about that in just a bit, but one night, long after I had stopped worrying about any police knocking on my door... there was a knock on my door. It was the police, with a warrant for my arrest. They had found the papers that had been hidden away.

By then, Pastor Larry Lea had taken over from Brother Howard. The moment he heard about my arrest, he immediately unleashed his thousands of prayer warriors on the Dallas court system.

On July 8, 1974, I went to stand in front of Judge R.T. Scales in the 195th Judicial Court. I had no doubt that Judge Scales was not happy with me. He said he was "going to put me away." I had already blown one probation, and he was ready to send me away. The District Attorney was even worse than the judge. The DA couldn't stand Lulu Roman, and he was going to make an example of her. Yes, Lulu was going to prison. There was no doubt about it.

But then, something very strange started happening. All these people began walking into the courtroom, and when it got full, even more people just started walking up and down the halls of the courthouse.

As they walked the halls, they prayed in tongues. The people in the courthouse had no idea what was happening, and the judge couldn't figure out what all these people were doing in his courtroom. When he asked me who they were, I quietly said, "I think they're from my church."

They just kept praying and praying. But on the day of my sentencing, I knew that I was going to prison. That was really the only option the judge had. So imagine my total astonishment when he told me he was giving me a ten year probated sentence. Everyone in the courtroom just gasped when he announced it. Including me.

Later, someone asked the judge why he had given me that probated sentence instead of sending me to prison. His only answer was, "I really don't know." But I knew, and everyone in my church knew. It was God.

Even though I was no longer on Hee Haw, my papa from the show, Sam Lovullo, had come to Dallas to support me. And the courts ended up putting me in Sam's custody for my probation. The judge named Sam as my guardian for the court.

My probation was not supposed to end until a decade later, on July 8, 1984… but in October of 1978, I received a true miracle from God. It came in the mail. I couldn't believe my eyes as I read a letter which stated, "Declaration: Setting aside judgement, dropping indictment, releasing defendant from probation."

Three and a half years into my ten year probation, I had been officially set free.

A short time later, my attorney Richard Worthy told me that I should ask for a full and complete pardon. We started the process by contacting everyone we knew, including religious leaders like Pat Robertson, Jim Bakker, Rex Humbard, who all sent letters, stating how I had turned my life around.

One of my probation officers even wrote a letter. She was a sweet little black lady named Connie. She wrote in her letter, "If everyone I have worked with would change their life and become the kind of person this young lady has become, this world would be a different and better place." It was so sweet of her.

Then my friend Dianne came up with the idea to ask the Governor for a pardon in person.

Dianne's maiden name happened to be Briscoe. The Texas Governor at the time was Dolph Briscoe. So Dianne and I drove from Dallas to Austin. We didn't make an appointment; we just showed up at the Governor's office. The governor's secretary asked our names, and we said, "Dianne Briscoe and Lulu Roman."

When she'd relayed our names to the Governor, of course he recognized my name, and I'm sure he was trying to remember how he was related to Dianne! After just a minute, the door opened, and the Governor smiled, "Come on in!"

I shared my story with Governor Briscoe. I told him about how I had been saved, and the work I was doing now in churches and prisons. I showed him letters that had been written on my behalf. The Governor said he was very confident that he could help me. He passed my request on to the incoming Governor, Bill Clements, and in 1981, I was granted a full and complete pardon by Governor Clements. The crime is not on my record anymore. My church, the Church on the Rock, held a "Pardon Sunday Celebration" for me. There were 7,000 people there that Sunday.

When I first got saved, the Reverend Rex Humbard called and asked me to come on his TV show and give my testimony. I told Dianne about it, and she said, "That is wonderful, Lou! You will be talking to millions of people."

I asked her "What is a testimony?"

"It's when you stand up and tell what the Lord has done for you. You just share your story. Tell them what you've been through."

When I started rehearsing my testimony in front of her, she yelled, "You can't tell that!" and "I'm pretty sure you shouldn't be telling ALL your story! Those church people will freak out! There are some things in your life those folks probably can't handle."

She helped me edit my testimony so that it wouldn't scare everyone to death!

On March 24, 1974, when I got to Rex Humbard's "Cathedral of Tomorrow" in Akron, Ohio, everyone treated me so great. I was so thrilled to meet Rex and his wife, Maude Aimee. I was extremely nervous, since it was the very first time I would be telling my story in front of such a huge television audience. Before I began talking, I asked the Lord to cover me, and I also asked him to watch over my mouth. My cussing like a sailor days were over, but I still sent up a prayer to just be sure!

I sang two songs on that show, "One Day Too Late" and "Now Let Me Sing". Then, for first time, I got up and gave my testimony. It was overwhelming. I was completely honest, and I held nothing back. After I gave my testimony, a large number of people got saved right then and there. Then Rex looked into the TV camera and said, "If you have been moved by Lulu's testimony, I want you to call this number." And their phone lines were jammed.

Later on, we received thousands letters from people who had gotten saved as they watched the show on TV. The Rex Humbard people sent huge mail bags full of letters to us. We would pour them out on the floor and read them, and we'd just cry.

After the service had ended, I went into Rex Humbard's office. Rex dropped onto his knees and prayed for me. He wept as he said, "Honey, today through the TV, you talked to more people than Jesus ever talked to."

I just cried. He continued, saying, "Lulu, you are a worldwide witness for our savior, as of this day."

It was at that moment that I knew I had found my true calling. I knew the reason I had felt unloved, unworthy and unwanted for my whole life. I knew that God had put me here so that I could help others who were dealing with those exact same feelings. I was put here to share the message that if you put your trust in the Lord, there is hope. No matter what you are going through, you can do this!

Rex Humbard had me on his show five years later. I sang three songs during the service, and afterward, Rex hugged me and said, "If you are ever going through a hard time, please call me. I don't care if

I'm in Russia or Tokyo, I will fly in to help you." I loved Rex so much. He was truly a man of God.

After my first appearance on Rex Humbard's show, people started calling me, asking me to come to their churches to give my testimony. I spoke in my first church in 1973, and I've averaged 2-3 churches a week since then. I've told my story thousands of times, in thousands of churches. I found that since I was so well known from Hee Haw, I was a pretty big draw to the church services. It seemed that everyone wanted to come see the fat, funny girl who was on TV.

The Lord gave me my testimony, and he also gave me my singing career. One time in church, a little gal named Linda Smith stood up and sang, "There's Something About That Name". She sang it acapella, and it moved me so much that I cried the entire way home. I finally pulled off on the side of the road and said, "Lord, that's what I want to do. I want to sing."

My wonderful Pastor Howard said to me, "Honey, if you want to sing, I'll let you sing."

When I first started singing, I was terrible! But I was singing for the Lord. That church let me get up front and sing and sing at each service. Brother Howard wouldn't let anyone in the congregation tell me that I wasn't very good yet, and the more I sang, the better I got.

Ironically, the man who had been the prosecuting attorney in my drug case also attended the very same church that I did. About six months after I'd started singing, he came up to me and smiled, saying, "I'm so glad that God has honored you. When you first started singing, honey, you were awful!"

I never had a voice lesson. I don't read music. It was totally the Lord who gave me this wonderful gift. I tell people who like to sing in the shower, "If you honor him, He will honor you."

The Lord blessed me, and the better I got, the more I praised God.

When I first started going out to sing in churches, I didn't have much of a wardrobe. I knew that my old hippie clothes just wouldn't cut it! But the grand lady of gospel came to my rescue; Vestal Goodman gave me one of her very own outfits. She was so sweet and so kind to me. For a long time, I wore that outfit almost every time I walked on stage.

Vestal and all of the gospel music people were very supportive of me as I began this unexpected new chapter of my life. They were just as wonderful to me as all of my Hee Haw friends were. They were very accepting. They gathered me up and welcomed me in.

In the spring of 1974, I received a call from Kathryn Kuhlman. Kathryn was a Pentecostal evangelist, and she was also a prophet. She held huge services and massive rallies. People would show up by the tens of thousands. Kathryn could wave her hand, and an entire section of the audience would go down. They all fell over! If she walked up and touched you, or waved her hand, you instantly hit the ground. When people hit the floor, they were said to have been "slain in the Spirit." I had no experience in the Spirit-filled life, and to be honest, it all kind of scared me.

My pastor, Brother Howard, told me about the time he had gone to Pittsburgh to see Kathryn Kuhlman. He had told everyone that he was not going to allow Kathryn to touch him, because he didn't want to fall for anyone. He went there, and Kathryn put him up on a platform with a big group of men. There were twenty preachers sitting in chairs across the stage, about twenty feet from her.

During the service, even though she wasn't close enough to touch them, she pointed to the group and then moved her hand, and every one of those pastors, including Brother Howard, fell right to the floor! She truly had an anointing that was not reasonable. It was more than frightening. It was beyond human knowledge.

All of that was going through my mind when they called to ask me to be on Kathryn's "I Believe in Miracles" program. I immediately said "No."

They called me again a week later, saying, "Mrs. Kuhlman would like you to be a guest on her show." Again, I turned them down.

A week later, a woman called and asked why I would not do the show. I said, "I ain't fallin' down for anybody."

A short time later, she called back and assured me that Mrs. Kuhlman had promised she would not touch me.

I asked Dianne to go on the program with me. Dino, the piano player who would later go on to make it big in Branson, was Kathryn's protégé when he was very young. Dino was also on the show.

When we walked into the studio on April 18, 1974, I made a point to sit as far across the set as I could from Kathryn. I did not want her to touch me and knock me out. I knew that if I passed out, they'd never get my big butt up off the floor! As we started the interview, Kathryn said, "Lulu, tell me what God has done for you."

At that point, I was a still baby Christian, and was just starting to know the Lord, but I began sharing my story and my testimony with her. As I told Kathryn about being abandoned when I was a little girl, she began to weep. She continued crying when I told her about the day after I'd gotten saved, and how I had no craving for the drugs I had been so heavily into.

I said, "When I gave my heart to Jesus, I was instantly delivered from drugs," and when I said the word 'instantly', I snapped my fingers. At that exact moment, Kathryn Kuhlman fell out! I sat there mortified. She was out! I couldn't believe it. But they got her up after a couple minutes. It was one of the most amazing experiences God has ever allowed me to have.

After the show, Katherine Kuhlman was just weeping. She said, "I've never been touched like this." She took Dianne by the hand, and she prayed over her. She prayed "that the gift of evangelism will absolutely overwhelm your life."

And it has. Everywhere Dianne goes, whether it's the grocery store or anywhere, God has brought people to her, and she has told them about Jesus... for the last 45 years! Those words that Kathryn prayed to Dianne were so powerful that they just went into her spirit.

On our way home, I decided to take Dianne over to the Hee Haw offices. I wanted to show some of the people there the 'new Lulu'. I wanted them to know that I had survived all my drug mess. When I walked into the Yongestreet offices, I saw Marsha, Sam Lovullo's secretary, at her desk.

I said, "Hi Marsha."

"Hello," she said back. I could tell she was looking at a stranger.

So again, I said, "Marsha!"

Again, she stared at me and said, "Yes."

I finally yelled, "Come on Marsha!"

"Lulu?!" She yelled out. My whole appearance had changed. I had cleaned up. I was not the hippie kid anymore.

Marsha ran and got Sam, Frank and John. Sam saw me and asked, "Lulu, what happened?" I told him the whole story, I said, "I got saved. I gave my heart to Jesus. He delivered me from drugs."

Tears just rolled down his cheeks. They were all so thrilled with how I looked. They asked what I had been doing, and I told them that I was singing in churches now. None of them could believe it! They all remembered my failed attempt to sing on Hee Haw a few years before. My song that never even got onto the air!

So John said, "Let me hear you sing."

I had a little portable tape player in the car, which housed a tape with the music track to "Blessed Assurance" on it. Dianne ran out and got the player. When she brought it in and pushed 'play', I knew everyone in that room was waiting to see what the punchline was to this joke I must be playing. But as I started to sing, they realized it was no joke. As I sang, each man had tears rolling down their cheeks. They were all crying. Sam was a Catholic, and Frank and John were Jewish, but they were all in tears.

At the end of my visit, Sam walked me out and whispered to me, "Lulu, we have gotten more fan mail about you than anyone else on Hee Haw. Will you come back to the show?"

I gave him my most honest answer. "I will pray about it, and if the Lord tells me to, I will."

A couple weeks later, Sam called and asked me again to come back onto the show. I told him that I would love to… on one condition. That was if they would let me sing my gospel music. Sam agreed.

But a short time later, he called and told me that, while the other producers would allow me to sing my music, they didn't want me to say "that name". I asked, "What name?"

He said, "You know…Jesus."

"Sam," I replied, "you tell those boys that I have a truckload of songs that say Lord and Savior and we'll be just fine."

When I returned to Hee Haw, I let the producers pick the first song they wanted me to sing… and ironically, they picked the same song I had sang for them with my little tape player. That song was "Blessed Assurance, JESUS is Mine"!

I sang my song, and the mail just poured in. People wanted to hear me sing… and sing my gospel music. My music was the first gospel music that was ever on Hee Haw, and when they saw how popular it was, they added the Hee Haw Gospel Quartet, which featured

Grandpa Jones, Buck Owens, Roy Clark and Kenny Price. I am so thankful to the Lord that He allowed Lulu Roman to be the person who brought gospel music to Hee Haw.

SAL-UTE!

When I returned to Hee Haw, many viewers hadn't even noticed that I had been away for a couple seasons. The way the show was edited allowed me to be away without many people missing me. Even a few of the cast members didn't know I hadn't been there. When we taped the show, we often didn't see the other folks who were not in our skits.

We filmed 13 Hee Haw shows each June, and then we did another 13 shows every October. Then they would re-run each of those shows one time, and that was an entire year's worth.

When we filmed the show, they would put up a different set, like the truck stop set, and we would shoot 13 different skits in the truck stop, one right after another. Then we'd change out our costumes and go over to another set and do 13 different skits there… and then we'd go to the third set and film another 13. All of that in one day.

That night, they'd rebuild the sets and maybe turn one into the Culhane Family set and another into the All Girl Jug Band set, and we'd come in and tape 13 of those skits, all in a row. And then finally at the end of the month, they would piece all of those different segments together into each show. They'd use that fast-paced editing style that the show became known for. We never saw the finished show until the public saw it on TV.

When we started doing the show, Cathy Baker and Larry Gatlin were painting the floors of the studio. They were both college students during the day, but at night they helped put together our sets. One of the producers saw Cathy and said, "That little gal who's painting the floor would make a great little girl next door for Hee Haw." They hired her, and she became known for ending each show with "That's all!"

But Larry Gatlin kept painting the floor! They didn't hire him. A few years later though, he was a star singing on the show! That's pretty unbelievable, and something even harder to believe is that Larry and I are distant cousins. My great grandmother was married to a Gatlin. When I told Larry that, he threw his arms wide open and screamed, "Cuz!"

We had to be on the set to put on our makeup at 6:30 each morning, and we'd start filming at 9:00. We never used a script. Instead, they had huge cue cards that they would hold up for us. We tried to read them over as quick as possible, to memorize them as best we could. But sometimes we'd have to glance over at them to get our line.

My favorite skit on Hee Haw was the truck stop. Not only did we get to eat the food, but we got to throw it. That was fun. I also loved the Culhanes, because they were so cornball.

When I started on Hee Haw, I made $600 a show. At its peak, they raised the pay to $1,200 a show. And we shot 26 episodes a year, so you can see that none of us got rich from Hee Haw. But we still get a little money from re-runs. They run from $200 to $700 once or twice a year.

One day, my son Damon was sitting in one of our living room chairs, and he asked me to come sit by him. I thought, "Oh boy, here it is. He's going to ask me about the birds and the bees."

I sat down with him, and he said, "Mom...we are going to watch Hee Haw."

We sat and watched the entire show, and at the end he said, "Wow. That is so silly."

"Well," I replied, "Gordie Tapp used to say, 'It's not silly. It's merely foolish.'"

In the first 25 years of Hee Haw, I didn't see more than 25 episodes of the show. I got so busy on the road singing that I just didn't have time to watch it. And even today, I have not seen all of the shows. There are many that I have never seen.

Besides me being busy on the road, there also is another reason I didn't watch the show. They say that television adds 25 to 30 pounds to you, and they are right! I couldn't take it! I was already so big, and when I saw myself on TV, I said, "I am not watching this."

I'm very thankful for everyone who still enjoys the shows today, but I can't stand to look at myself when I was so fat.

After each month of filming, we would all go our separate ways again. Since we only taped the show two times a year, each time we would come in to shoot, it was like old home week. We all caught each other up on what was happening in our lives. We really became a large, loving family... the first family I had really had. All those people were so good and so nice to me. They have all been lifelong, loving friends.

I never saw anyone in our cast having a fight with someone else. I never saw anyone being rude or ugly to anyone else. We really were a wonderful family. I loved everyone on there. I really did. I could sit down and talk to any of them about things that I would never talk to anyone else about. They loved me unconditionally. I had never had that in my life.

Since I'm talking about the cast, I'd like to share a few of my memories about some of my Hee Haw family members:

Buck Owens: Buck was a good man. He was so good to me. Without him, no one would have ever heard of me. He was the one who'd put the money on the girl. He was the one who believed in me. If Buck hadn't called me to come and be on Hee Haw... I think I would probably be dead.

Buck died on March 25, 2006. I sang at his funeral in Bakersfield. Buck had planned all of his funeral out. Dwight Yoakam sang. Garth Brooks, Trace Atkins and Brad Paisley were also there. But I was the only woman who he wanted to sing. He requested that I sing "Amazing Grace". And I did. Buck always told me "Amazing Grace" was his mama's favorite song, and that I was her favorite singer.

At the end of my song, I went over to his casket and whispered, "I love you Buck. I will see you again. And oh my, we will sing together... again."

Roy Clark: Roy Clark and I were the two people who got the most fan mail. I got many, many marriage proposals in the mail. A lot of those came from prisoners. I still have bags and bags of fan mail that I have saved over the years.

I am so proud that Roy Clark loved Jesus. He really loved Jesus. Roy Clark, Roy Acuff and Kenny Price all shared their faith. If they were asked, they would always say "Yes, I am a Christian." They were not ashamed to tell you. Grandpa and Ramona Jones, Stringbean, and the Hager Brothers were all Christians. The Hagers' father was a Methodist preacher. A lot of the cast and crew went to church every Sunday. I'd say that at least 90% of the people who worked on Hee Haw were Christians. There were only a few who weren't.

I was working on this book when I got word that Roy Clark was near death. He had not been well for the past year, but it was still a shock when he passed away on November 15, 2018. Roy was 85 years old, but he always seemed so much younger. I was heartbroken when Roy died, but I have no doubt of where he is now. When the good Lord uses Cathy Baker's line on me and says, "That's All!", I look forward to seeing Roy, and so many other dear friends, once again in Heaven.

Grandpa Jones: Grandpa was precious. He was sweet and so kind. But you did not want to make him mad. If he got mad, look out. But he was so funny.

Grandpa was hard of hearing, and he talked loud. One day, we were sitting on the couch, getting ready to shoot a Culhanes skit, and Misty Rowe and Gunilla Hutton walked by in their short shorts. Grandpa thought he was whispering, but he very loudly said, "If I walked like that, I would walk everywhere I went."

This is a little risqué, but so was Grandpa, so forgive me. I had a silver Lincoln Continental, and Grandpa loved it. I told him the dealership where I'd bought it from, and he went down to buy one just like mine. When he got there, he was walking through the lot and one of the salesmen came out and asked him, "Grandpa, are you looking for anything in particular?"

Grandpa said, "Well, I'm-a lookin' for some pu--y… but I am gonna buy a car!"

Junior Samples: I've already talked a little about Junior, but there is so much more to tell! I loved Junior Samples. He was very sweet. There will never be another one like him.

It would be easy to say that Junior Samples never changed, even though he had gone from a drunk fisherman to a TV star. But Junior did in fact change… in a very good way.

Junior had heart problems. He had phlebitis real bad in his legs. They always let Junior and I sit in rocking chairs. They knew that neither one of us could stand for a long time, so they'd let us sit and rock.

One day, in between takes, when we were the only two around, Junior turned to me and said, "Miss Lulu, I ain't gonna be on this earth long."

I said, "Honey, can I ask you a question? Has anybody ever told you about Jesus?"

I will never forget how his eyes filled with tears, and as he began to weep, Junior said, "I could show you the rock I was sittin' on when the Lord saved me."

He told me how he had stopped drinking over the last year. He went on to say how he'd told the Lord, "All I ask is, if you'll let me build a home for each of my children, I will give you my life and I will serve you." And Junior had built a home with his own hands for every one of his six kids!

I just cried and hugged his neck. I said, "You know that you and I will see each other again in Heaven."

He smiled and said, "Yes ma'am."

When you are on TV, or if you're a music star, fans and regular people can lose their minds over you. People also go crazy over anyone who has money, and when Junior came into money, he had more girls hanging around him! He just smiled his good ole boy smile at each one. I'm sure if any of those women had wanted to go fishin', Junior would have been glad to take them!

Junior died of a heart attack on November 14, 1983. He was just 57 years old. I sang "Amazing Grace" at his funeral. He was wearing his overalls in the casket. His wife Grace and his kids were so heartbroken. So was I. But I know he is catching the world's biggest whopper in Heaven.

Archie Campbell: Archie Campbell was very, very funny. He was funny on screen and behind the scenes, he was also a jokester… some might call him a dirty old man.

Archie would walk up and tap anybody in the crotch. It didn't matter if it was a man or a woman. He was just playing. But he'd lightly flick your private area with his hand and he'd say, "Take a bow."

He did that to me just one time. It was during the first year of Hee Haw, before I got saved. He walked up and flicked my private area, and before he knew what hit him, I grabbed a handful of his crotch and said, "You take a bow." He never touched me again!

Kenny Price: They called Kenny Price the "Round Mound of Sound". He stood 6 foot tall and weighed 300 pounds, so I could relate very well to him! Kenny was a good guy, and I just loved him. He was so sweet, and he was one of the funniest men I ever met.

Kenny did a skit where he'd appear before the judge Archie Campbell. Every now and then, as he stood there, his pants would start falling down, and he'd stand there in his underwear as the entire studio exploded into laughter.

In 1978 and '79, they did a spinoff of Hee Haw called Hee Haw Honeys. It was Sam Lovullo's idea. Kenny Price played Kenny Honey, and I was Lulu Honey, and we had three children. One was Gailard Sartain, and the other two were Misty Rowe and Kathie Lee Johnson, who later became Kathie Lee Gifford.

Kenny and I played cooks in the show. We had a restaurant, and the kids worked there. We had guest stars who'd come in and sing. It was a nice show, and it did real well. But eventually, Sam pulled it off the air, because he didn't want it to compete against Hee Haw. We filmed the show in Nashville, and Kathie Lee and I became very good friends. She is a sweet Christian woman.

Kenny had a powerful relationship with God. He and I had many wonderful talks about our faith, and how the Lord was working in our lives. Kenny made sure he passed that faith on to his children. He worked hard so that his daughter could go to college. She went on to marry a minister, and Kenny sent his son to seminary, where he served the Lord through music.

In 1987, Kenny and I started working together on a duet album. We were going to sing the duets on Hee Haw, but we had only three of the songs done when Kenny had a heart attack in Florence, Kentucky. He died on August 4, 1987, at the very young age of just

56. I'm sure he'll be waiting to sing a duet with me when I get to Heaven.

Minnie Pearl: When she put on that hat with the price tag, she became Minnie Pearl. But when she took it off, she was Sarah Ophelia Colley Cannon. In real life, Sarah was very sophisticated and classy, but when she put that hat on, she could get country in a heartbeat.

We were once filming a day of skits with the All Girl Jug Band. I blew into my moonshine jug, and Minnie Pearl played the piano. In between takes, however, I noticed that Minnie was crying. I watched her for about ten minutes, and then when we went into our dressing room, I asked her if she was OK.

She said, "I have done the Grand Ole Opry with Roy Acuff for 50 years, and in all those years, Roy has never given me an autographed photo. But today, he came down the hall and he had an 8x10 photo, and he had written on it, 'To Miss Minnie, my friend. I love you. Roy Acuff'. It touched her heart so much that she couldn't stop crying.

As Hee Haw was winding down, we could kind of feel that our days were coming to an end. Some of the girls in the cast thought it would be a good idea for us to take Miss Minnie out to lunch as often as we could. We weren't going for the food; we were going to hear all of her stories! She had the greatest stories.

She told us how she'd met her husband. She had gone to an officer's party, and Henry Cannon walked in. He was a fly boy. And he walked up to her and said, "Sarah Ophelia, you are the prettiest girl I have ever seen, and someday I am going to marry you."

She responded, "Get away from me. I don't even know you."

But he came back again later and said the same thing, and again she sent him away. A short time later, he came back with the exact same message, and he received the same response. But at the end of the evening, he walked up to her one last time, and said, "Sarah, go get your coat."

For some reason, she did, and they were never apart again.

Roy Acuff: Mr. Acuff was so precious. He would sit with me on the side of the set. All he wanted to do was talk about Jesus. I can't tell you what an honor it was for me to talk with Roy about our faith. He was so ready to go and be with Jesus. He wanted to go a long time before he went.

I sang a song on Hee Haw called "That's the Man I'm Looking For", and when I finished, Roy Acuff walked up to me and said, "That's the prettiest song I've ever heard. Do you reckon I could sing it?"

"Sweetheart," I replied, "your name is Roy Acuff. I reckon you can sing anything you wanted to."

Mr. Acuff asked if I could get him a tape of the song, and I responded, "I sure can. But I'd like something in return." I had remembered how touched Minnie Pearl had been when Roy gave her an autographed photo, so I told Roy, "I'll get you a tape of the song, but I'd like a signed picture of you."

A couple days later, Mr. Acuff brought me an 8x10 photo, inscribed: 'To Lulu with love and friendship, Roy Acuff'. I treasure that photo.

I got to sing "That's the Man I'm Looking For" with Roy on Hee Haw, and also on the Grand Ole Opry. From that day on, he sang that song every time he performed on the Opry. I just love that Roy Acuff loved my song so much. He sang it until the day he went running into the arms of Jesus.

Charlie McCoy: I love Charlie McCoy. He was booked to play harmonica behind Ray Charles on Hee Haw. When Sam Lovullo saw how great he was, he called Charlie and asked if he would consider being a part of the band each week. He joined the show in season seven, and stayed on until the very end.

Charlie is so awesome. He is so sharp. No matter what your musical need is, he can do it. He is like fine wine. The older he gets, the better he gets. He is one of the true legends in Nashville.

I did a guest spot on Charlie's first gospel album. We were supposed to do a show together in Florida this past year, but I had to cancel. I was looking forward to being with him, and hopefully we can do a show or two sometime soon.

Tennessee Ernie Ford: Ernie was a good man. He was already a TV and country music legend before he came to Hee Haw. Of course, his song "Sixteen Tons" is a classic.

Tennessee Ernie was so sweet to me. I had just started singing, and was still very nervous. One day, after I'd finished a song on the show, I walked backstage and Tennessee Ernie was there, talking to Jimmy Dean. Ernie yelled, "Come here little girl! You have got such a great voice."

Jimmy Dean said, "Yes you do. You are really going to be something special." I might have weighed over 300 pounds, but I went home floating on air.

Gordie Tapp: Gordie was something else. He was a jokester, he could tell 200 jokes in two minutes. He knew so many jokes. Gordie was a good guy. He was also very smart, just sharp as a tack. On top of this, he was a fabulous writer, and he wrote a lot of the jokes on Hee Haw.

One day when Gordie was doing his judge skit, he was supposed to hit Archie Campbell over the head with a rubber chicken. Archie always wore a toupee, and when Gordie popped him, that rubber chicken stuck to Archie's wig and pulled it straight up! That was one blooper that wasn't allowed to go on the air.

Gordie could play a southern hillbilly… but he was actually from Canada! He was a big star there. He died on December 18, 2016 at the age of 94.

Don Harron: Everyone remembers his silly newsman "Charlie Farquharson" on KORN radio on Hee Haw. But like Gordie, Don was also from Canada! And he was a very popular actor there. He was quite educated, very smart. He was quiet, but he was funny.

Don lived in Canada throughout the run of the show, and he would fly into Nashville, do his thing, and then head right back. We didn't get to spend a lot of time with him. He didn't stay for all of the taping sessions like some of us did. But he was a nice guy.

Gailard Sartain: There never was, and never will be, another like Gailard. He is such a great actor. He had impeccable timing, and he was very smart. He is brilliant. He was a great character actor, and he went on to appear in many movies after Hee Haw.

Gailard's facetime grew with each season of the show, because everyone could see that he was so funny. He is one of the funniest guys I have ever met in my life. Off screen, he wasn't all that jovial, but when that camera turned on, he just lit up.

I loved doing the truck stop skit, with Gailard as the cook and me as the waitress. By the way, I still have my waitress outfit. I also have my dress from the Culhanes sketch. I have my Hee Haw overalls, and I have the shirt that I wore in the cornfield. It has cutoffs and lace around the top. I saved my shoes, and my hat and bows that I wore on the show. I also have the huge Hee Haw donkey that they used on the set.

The Hager Brothers: The Hager Twins were so great. They were funny and wonderful. A lot of teenage girls tuned in to see the Hagers on Hee Haw in the 70s. I did many live shows on the road with the Hagers. Like me, Jim and Jon had also been orphans. But they were adopted by a couple in Chicago.

We also had another thing in common: Jon and Jim had also been discovered by Buck Owens. Buck had seen them performing at Disneyland, and told the Hee Haw producers they should sign them.

In 1973, the Hager Brothers appeared in the second issue of Playgirl Magazine! They were both standing on haystacks, without a stich of clothes on! It looked like they were on the Hee Haw set! Thankfully, Jim's guitar was covering his private parts... just barely!

Jim and Jon Hager were always in good shape, both very thin. But Jon had a heart problem. Everyone knew about it. But on May 1, 2008, his brother Jim dropped dead from a heart attack. He was only 66 years old. No one, including him, even knew he had any heart trouble. His brother Jon was absolutely heartbroken. He never got over Jim's death, and eight months later, Jon died in his sleep.

Cathy Baker: Cathy was the always-smiling, blonde little girl who ended each show with her signoff, "That's all!" Today, Cathy is my best friend from Hee Haw. She is probably my closest friend from the show.

She lives in Virginia, where she works in her ex-husband's law office. Any time I'm traveling near her home, I like to spend a day or two with her. She knows almost everything about me, and she still loves me!

Gunilla Hutton: Nurse Good Body! And Gunilla still has a very good body! She is still one of my dearest friends. Gunilla is a very classy woman.

Misty Rowe: Misty was, and still is, a sweetheart. She has always been very talented. Misty was so great with Junior Samples in his BR-549 used car sketches. "Misty's Bedtime Stories" was a popular segment on the show. Scot England, the man who helped me write this book, is such a fan of Misty's that he bought the bed she did all of her bedtime stories in. He still has it today!

George Lindsey: George Lindsey had already become typecast as Goober on the Andy Griffith Show. When that show ended, he couldn't get any acting jobs, because everyone saw him as Goober. So he really resented Goober for a long time... but then he decided that he might as well embrace it. So he brought his Goober character to Hee Haw, and he was Goober until the day he died.

George was precious. When they first brought him in, some people were not sure if they wanted him in with us, but he just slid right in and took his place, and became a huge part of the show. He was a good man and a real sweetheart.

In late 2011, Larry Black put together a Hee Haw reunion. He called it "Salute to the Kornfield". The special aired on RFD, and featured almost every cast member who was still alive. It was such a special day that I will never forget. Everybody just sat around and talked about the good ol' days.

We all knew that George Lindsey had been very sick. I had heard he was near death, so none of us thought he would be there... but just as we started taping, George walked in. He had come straight from the hospital. He had somehow willed himself up. George died just a short time later, on May 6, 2012. He passed away on my birthday.

Roni Stoneman: Roni was known for her banjo playing and her missing front teeth! Roni is a rebel. If she's in the room, she's usually the center of attention. She is one of the most gifted banjo players I've ever seen in my life.

Lisa Todd: Lisa was the buxom weather girl on Hee Haw. Lisa was a strange little bird. She used to do chants during our lunch break. But she was very talented. She lives in New York, and is married to a doctor.

Buck Trent: Buck is wonderful. Before joining Hee Haw, he was with the Porter Wagner and Dolly Parton show. Buck's a heck of a banjo player. He is so good. After Hee Haw, he made it big with his own show in Branson, Missouri. He still plays Branson today, and I still go to see him any time I can. I love him.

Marianne Gordon: Marianne is so sweet. She was so genuine. She was the epitome of southern class. One of her sketches had her playing a rich, southern belle. In 1976, Kenny Rogers made his first appearance on Hee Haw. And while he was on the set, he met Marianne, and they started dating. A year later, Marianne married Kenny, and became Marianne Rogers. They were married for 15 years. When they divorced, Kenny had to pay Marianne 60 million dollars! So, she can probably relate to that rich, southern belle role!

Linda Thompson: Linda Thompson was Elvis' girlfriend for four years. She was still with Elvis when she became a Hee Haw honey. Linda and I were real good friends when we were doing the show. She told me that Elvis loved Hee Haw, and that he loved MY music!

During our taping in June of 1977, Linda told me that Elvis wanted her to bring me to Graceland, so we made plans for me to go when we got together for our next taping in October. But Elvis died in August, so I missed out on my meeting with him at Graceland.

Wouldn't it have been something if Elvis would have done Hee Haw? The closest we got was when Linda Thompson had Elvis' father on the show. Vernon appeared on Hee Haw right after Elvis died. It was kind of a strange deal. You could tell Vernon was just heartbroken, and you could also see how sad the entire cast was. It was the one show where we weren't joking and laughing at the end.

Diana Goodman: Diana was a Hee Haw Honey. She had also dated Elvis for a very short time. It was a little uncomfortable on the set when she was there with Linda Thompson, but they both handled it very well. There would be no cat fight in Kornfield Kounty!

Barbi Benton: Barbi was on Hee Haw for four years. She wanted to be a country singer, and she did have a little success with a couple records, but her biggest success came as a model for Playboy

Magazine! Not only did she appear in the magazine many times, but she was also the girlfriend of the Playboy founder, Hugh Hefner.

Barbi actually talked Hugh into appearing on Hee Haw. He didn't really do anything on the show, but he did wear his robe and pajamas! When I first met Barbi, I didn't think she was all that beautiful. She looked more like the girl next door. But I had never seen her without her clothes on! Barbi was a nice girl, and she has always been very sweet to me.

Victoria Hallman: Victoria played Miss Honeydew in a skit with Minnie Pearl. She had originally been a female vocalist with Buck Owens' Buckaroos. This past year, Victoria and Diana Goodman teamed up to write a book about the Hee Haw years. I hope it sells a million copies… and I hope mine outsells theirs!

Jana Jae: Jana is one of the nicest people you will ever meet. Buck Owens discovered Jana, and brought her to the show. She came in as part of his band. When she started playing her blue fiddle, we all thought that she was awesome. Buck and Jana ended up getting married, but that lasted only a few days! They had their marriage annulled.

In late 2018, Jana helped put together a live show called "Kornfield Friends". It included Jana, Misty Rowe, Buck Trent, and me. We all told stories and did our own music. We had a question and answer session with the audience, and we also paid tribute to all of our Hee Haw family members who have passed on.

Stringbean: String was a member of the Grand Ole Opry. His real name was David Akeman. He played the banjo, and was a comedian. He played the scarecrow in the cornfield on Hee Haw. He was precious. He was very quiet, and quite smart. But when he opened his mouth, he would make you laugh.

On November 10, 1973, Stringbean was murdered as he came home after playing the Opry. He was known for carrying a lot of cash.

He didn't believe in banks, and he kept big wads of money in his overalls. Two men killed Stringbean, and as his wife begged for her life, they shot and killed her too.

Stringbean's death devastated all of us, especially Grandpa Jones, who was his best friend. Grandpa is also the one who found the bodies of Stringbean and his wife.

String's death was one of the first that our Hee Haw family would have to go through over the run of the show.

We mourned those deaths like any family would. When we returned to Nashville to film the show two times a year, it was always like a big family reunion when we all got back together. We'd catch each other up on what was happening in our lives. During those first years, we'd celebrate weddings as people got married. Then as the years went on, we'd celebrate babies and children that everyone had. But as the years continued, we had to mourn the passing of many of the cast members and their families. We all just went through everything that a real family deals with in their lives. Life, and death, and the whole circle.

Jeff Smith: Jeff was one of the Hee Haw Hunks that joined the show later in its run. Jeff was young and good lookin'. He could usually be found in the haystack with Linda Thompson. He was no fool! Jeff is now a minister of music at a church in North Carolina.

Mackenzie Colt: Mackenzie was a Hee Haw Honey for six years. But when she was not on the set, she was starting her life as an entrepreneur. She turned her love of chocolate into a very successful business. As she was trying to invent the perfect combination of chocolate and peanut butter, she invited all of us Hee Haw girls over to her apartment, where she melted different combinations of chocolate and had us as her "taste testers"! I loved it all! Mackenzie eventually came up with a candy that she named "Colts Bolts", and it became very popular. Today, she still runs her Colts Chocolates

Company in Nashville. If you want to taste a little piece of Heaven, you need to take a nibble of one of Mackenzie's "Colts Bolts".

The Nashville Edition: Our backup vocal group was so much more! In addition to being a huge part of Hee Haw, the Nashville Edition also sang on almost every country music album that was released in the 1960s and 70s. During that time, the Nashville Edition appeared on more than 12,000 recordings! Joe Babcock, Ricki Page, Dolores Edgin and Hurshel Wiginton were the original members of the group. Wendy Suits took over from Ricki Page after a couple seasons of Hee Haw. Sadly, Wendy died in 2013. Dolores passed away in 2015, and Hurshel died two years later. I still work with Joe Babcock quite often, especially on the show he started called "Sunday Morning Country". That concert at the Grand Ole Opry House always closes out the CMA Fest activities each June.

There is one more Hee Haw cast member that I get asked about quite often... and that is the long eared bloodhound! We actually had four different dogs over the two and a half decades of the show. The first one was named "Kingfish", but he tragically choked on a bone just one year into the show. Then we got "Beauregard the Wonder Dog". He was on the show with us for five years, and he stank a little more with each passing year! He was replaced by "Beauregard, Jr.". They weren't actually related. Jr. ran away after four years. Our last bloodhound was named "Buford". And while "Beauregard" stunk to high heaven, we all wanted him back, after we found out that "Buford" like to pass gas... all day long!

Our set was most like a family when its creators, Frank Peppiatt and John Aylesworth, were still with the show. They sent us Christmas gifts every year. They gave all the cast members wonderful gifts, and when holidays came around, they threw big parties. They had huge Thanksgiving dinners for us. But when they sold Hee Haw and Gaylord took over, things changed, and our family atmosphere was never quite the same.

I am still dear friends with Cathy Baker, Misty Rowe, Gunilla Hutton, and Victoria Hallman. I love them. We have all gotten closer as the years have gone by. So many of our Hee Haw family members have died. As you lose people, that kind of bonds the ones who are still here even tighter.

When we were taping Hee Haw in October of 1978, someone in the cast came up and asked me, "How about that baby that was named after you?"

On July 25, 1978, the world's first "test tube baby" was born in Oldham, England. Even though they had called her a test tube baby, she was actually conceived in a Petri dish! The little girl was named Louise Joy Brown, and they had given her the nickname of "Lulu"! Most people didn't think Louise "Lulu" Brown would live. But as I write this, she is now 40 years old!

And Hee Haw, the show that all the critics said would never last... ran for 25 years! But in 1993, I woke up one morning and saw a TV news report that Hee Haw had been cancelled. I was on the first Hee Haw show, and I was on the last show. I probably laughed more in those two decades than I have laughed in all of my other years of life total.

If you ever watched an episode of Hee Haw, I thank you. Every time you reached out and turned your television to Hee Haw, you were giving me my life. You were helping all of my dreams come true. I love you for watching the show. I will always be grateful to you.

BE OUR GUEST

When Hee Haw first went on the air, I didn't know anything about Country Music. But I quickly fell in love with it. Then I fell in love with the people who were in Country Music. The same thing happened to me with Gospel music. I fell in love with the music first, and that led to my love for the people who made the music.

During its quarter-century on the air, Hee Haw brought country music to a national audience. This was before cable television, and even after the show was cancelled by CBS, Hee Haw's TV audience in syndication was just huge. The show was really one of the very few places where country fans could see their favorite artists.

Almost every country legend appeared on the show. Hee Haw was also known as being the first big TV exposure for many country newcomers who would go on to become huge stars. For those performers just starting out, Hee Haw was a big goal that they dreamed of. A little piece of trivia for you... in 1969, each guest artist was paid $1,000 to be on Hee Haw. Every performer got that, whether they were a huge star or a newcomer, and 25 years later, each guest artist still got the exact same $1,000!

Here are a few of my memories of some of those legends and newcomers.

Johnny Cash: Johnny Cash did a couple Hee Haw shows. In 1974, he came on the show. He knew all about my story. He knew my drug history, and he also knew that I had been born again. He could relate to all of that. We had so much in common. Johnny took the time to sit and talk with me on the set. He sat there with me for forty-five minutes, and we talked about Jesus. It was just me and him.

Johnny talked about dreams he had at night, and how God interpreted them for him. He told me what God was doing in his life, and he talked about how much he loved Jesus. I was so impressed with him. When I first heard that he got saved, I wondered how sincere he was, but I soon found out that he was truly saved. Johnny was the one star who impressed me more than any other. He wasn't afraid to tell you about his walk with Jesus. I loved Johnny Cash.

George Jones/Tammy Wynette: George and Tammy were on many Hee Haw shows. George was on as a solo act, and Tammy was also on by herself. Then they came on as a duet. They were on throughout the entire run of the show. During that period, they went from being popular singers to being true superstars, and they still kept coming on Hee Haw!

Tammy and I used to say that we were twins from different mothers. Her birthday was May 5th, and mine is May 6th. We were so much alike. You couldn't tell it by looking at us, but we really were.

And George Jones loved my big boobs! I always laughed when his eyes just lit up when he saw me and my big boobs walking toward him! He would come at me with his arms wide open, just a-grinnin'.

Garth Brooks: Garth Brooks is so precious. I met Garth many, many years ago. Dottie West, Garth and I played a show in Texas. It was way before Garth got famous.

Garth sang on Hee Haw for the first time in 1990, and he did four Hee Haw shows over the next two years. Today, any time Garth sees me, he just hugs me and treats me so nice. We are friends, and he has always been so good to me. He is such a sweetheart, so genuine and kind. He always takes his hat off when he comes up to hug me. I love Garth Brooks. He is just one of the very best.

Tanya Tucker: Tanya was just 13 years old when she sang "Delta Dawn" on Hee Haw! Since that day, Tanya and I have always been good friends. We were both always wild and crazy, and we have lived to tell about it!

Dolly Parton: Dolly has just been like a sister to me. When you have a sister who you love very deeply, even if you don't get to see each other very often, when you do, it's like you've never been away from each other. She has always been very sweet and very respectable to me, and I've always tried to give that back to her. I love Dolly.

Loretta Lynn: Loretta Lynn was one of those performers who always came on Hee Haw, no matter how big of a superstar she had become. She also sang with Conway Twitty on a number of our shows. Loretta has always been very sweet to me. I played a concert with Loretta, Dolly and Dottie West at the Nashville Municipal Auditorium. We all shared a dressing room together. It was quite a night.

Jerry Lee Lewis: Jerry Lee was crazy! When he came on the show, he had big demands and a team of lawyers, and no one was real happy with him.

Randy Travis: In 1989, Randy Travis and Merle Haggard did Hee Haw. They don't come any bigger or better than that. Randy is still a dear friend today. I put together and hosted a fundraiser in April of 2018 for the Randy Travis Foundation, where we raised over ten thousand dollars. His foundation raises money for stroke victims, as well as to give musical instruments to underprivileged children. We plan on hosting our fundraising show each year to help Randy and his organization. He and his wife Mary are dear, dear friends, and I love them both with an undying love!

I have many other favorites who performed on Hee Haw. Lorrie Morgan was on quite a few times. She is so funny and so sweet. She has always been so wonderful to me. Lorrie is a class act on stage, and she is an even classier friend. I love her so much. She is one of my favorite people, and I was so thrilled when she agreed to do the foreword for my book!

Mel Tillis was always the consummate performer. He was also a gentleman. He was a remarkable and precious spirit. He always gave me a big hug, every time that he saw me. Mel always wanted to share his stage with others. I went to see his show when I was on vacation, and when he saw me out in the audience, he pulled me up on stage to sing. He joked that he wanted a break.

One of my very favorite people is **Jan Howard**. I love her strength and resilient spirit. She is my hero. I had the honor of inducting Jan into the Cherry Blossom Festival Hall of Fame in Missouri, and she is one of the greatest people I have ever met in my whole life. She is awesome. You don't mess with Jan. She has lived through some of the hardest times you can ever imagine. I want to hang out with her any time I can. I love and adore Jan Howard!

I also loved **Jim Ed Brown**. He was such a sweet man. I went in to see Jim Ed Brown just before he died; I walked into his hospital room, and he said, "There's my beautiful redhead." I sang to him, and then he sang with me, right in his hospital bed. His sisters were there too, and it was truly a precious time.

Yes, Hee Haw was known for its Country Music stars… but it also hosted a lot of stars from other walks of life. Here are a few people whom I would have never dreamed would have stepped foot on the Hee Haw set:

Sammy Davis Jr. – One of the greatest moments of my life came in 1982, when they put me in the cornfield with Sammy Davis Jr.! Sammy was known for wearing all kinds of jewelry, and he kept all his rings and necklace on when he was on the show, even though he was wearing overalls! When we got into the cornfield, I started taking his rings off his fingers, one at a time, and I put them onto my hand. I dropped one ring down my shirt, and said, "You've got to come and get it." And he did! Sammy was wonderful. I loved him so much.

Ernest Borgnine – I knew Ernest very well. He was best friends with George Lindsey. George had asked him to do the show, and Ernest ended up doing a few of them. He was so great, and was such a cut-up. He had a lovely wife named Tova, who had brought all the Hee Haw Honeys some very nice perfume. All of us girls smelled glorious! Ernest was a sweetheart.

Ethel Merman – "There's No Business Like Show Business!" She did the show in 1980. The other guest that night was Kenny Rogers. I loved Ethel. She was so out there with her over-the-top voice. I could relate to her.

Ed McMahon – What the heck was Johnny Carson's sidekick doing in the cornfield?! He was probably thinking the same thing! But Ed came in, and loved it so much that he started hanging around as much as he could. He kind of blended in with the furniture as he watched the show behind the scenes. He was a nice man.

John Ritter – John was the son of country great Tex Ritter, but in 1977, he became one of the biggest stars on TV, with his show "Three's Company". He was so hot when he agreed to be on a Hee Haw in 1978. John was so great. He was such a sweetheart. He was so kind and so funny. He knew how to treat people, he really did.

Billy Carter – In 1977, Jimmy Carter was the President of the United States. I have no doubt that Jimmy loved Hee Haw. He probably watched it every week. But we still couldn't get the President on the show. We did get his brother though! To be honest, I didn't really get to know Billy. But he quickly made friends with all of the men on the show because he brought in cases of his Billy Beer.

Amanda Blake – She was Miss Kitty on "Gunsmoke". She was also very popular when she appeared on our show in 1971, and viewers were so surprised to hear her sing "Your Cheatin' Heart" and "Oh Lonesome Me". I loved Amanda. We got along so well. She was a tough redhead who talked with this husky voice. I was enamored with her, because she had the ability to be rough, and also be a lady at the same time. We became very good friends, and I just loved her.

Mickey Mantle – Mickey appeared on the same episode as Amanda Blake. Mickey was a really nice guy. He became very close with Roy Clark, and Roy sang his song, "Yesterday When I was Young", at Mickey's funeral.

Johnny Bench – Johnny was another baseball player who wanted to be on Hee Haw. He was so fun. Johnny and Mickey Mantle both brought in baseballs to sign for the cast. Johnny liked to hang out with us. He ate lunch with everyone, and he actually sang a song on the show, Jim Croce's "You Don't Mess Around with Jim". It is a true classic.

GLOOM, DESPAIR, AND AGONY ON ME

Life was always fun in the cornfield. But TV is not real life, and the real life of Lulu Roman always seemed filled with so much drama.

Remember my son's father, John? We never married, and John ran off as soon as he found out I was pregnant.

When Damon was 11 years old, my phone rang. It was John. He had been gone for more than a decade, but he acted just like nothing had ever happened. He acted like he had no idea he'd missed the first ten years of his son's life. Then he asked to see Damon again.

I said, "Alright. But don't come over and act like you are going to just move in like old times."

By then, I was a completely different person. I had gotten saved, and was no longer doing drugs. When John came back onto the scene, we didn't renew our relationship… but he continued to come in and out of our lives over the years, and he was somehow able to build a pretty good relationship with Damon. They got to know each other, and they were able to become a real father and son, and it turned into a good thing.

John ended up marrying another woman, and they had a son together as well. So my son Damon has a brother, but he has never been able to find out who he is, or where he is. John died a couple years ago. I am so thankful that my son got to have a relationship with his father. John and I always told each other that we'd be best friends for the rest of our lives, and we were. John was the love of my life.

When I was not filming on Hee Haw, I was on the road speaking in every church that asked me to come. And boy, did they ask!

Hee Haw gave me the visibility to be able to go out and sing and share my testimony across the country. My fame from the show gave me the opportunity to draw a crowd, so that I could show them what God can do in somebody's life.

When I arrived at each church, I always knew what I would see on the sign outside: it was always "Lulu Roman from Hee Haw". It was like Lulu was my first name, with Roman being my middle name, and 'from Hee Haw' being my last name. I never cared. If that's what it took for me to get a crowd to hear my story, then I was all for it.

I had many interesting experiences during my church travels. One of those came when I was ministering in a large church in Shreveport, Louisiana. I was not real familiar back then with people who talk in tongues. I had not grown up with that kind of worship.

I was sitting in the pastor's office as I was preparing to go out and speak, and the more I sat and prayed, the more I began to realize that I was very quietly worshipping in tongues. All of a sudden, I thought, "I must be standing before the throne of God!"

I had the wherewithal to look around me then, and saw that there was no one else there. I was the only one. I know that I didn't see the face of God, but I saw a light that was hitting me, and bouncing off and hitting me again, as I talked in tongues. Finally, the pastor walked in and tapped me on the shoulder and asked if I was OK. It was an experience I will never forget.

During the first year I was on Hee Haw, long before I had gotten saved, I was a potty-mouthed drug addict. I lived in a little apartment in Dallas, and one day when I got mad, I shot my television! I think I'd heard that Elvis liked to shoot his TVs. Of course, he could afford to go out and buy another one. I couldn't.

So I called the TV repair shop, and they sent a little guy over to fix my television. His name was Mose Cummins. When he walked in, he said, "Lou, you know that Jesus loves you. He wants you to be his."

I looked at him and screamed, "F--- you! Just fix my TV!"

Moe just smiled as he took my TV away.

A week later, Mose brought my TV back. As he hooked it up, he looked at me and said, "Lou, Jesus loves you so much, honey. You know Jesus loves you. He wants you to be his."

I yelled "F--- you! And f--- your Jesus! Get out!"

When I gave my heart to Jesus though, I led a Jesus March down the streets of Dallas. One of Mose' daughters saw me on the news then, and called him. He didn't believe her. He said it had to be someone else.

A short time later, one Sunday night, I was singing at the Beverly Hills Baptist Church, when I saw Mose walking down the aisle. He had a smile a mile long, and we had a glorious reunion. Mose had his 10 year old son Dan with him as well, and Dan and I became good friends. He grew up to be a pastor. Their family had a great impact on my life.

I had another, even more surprising reunion in Commerce, Texas. I was performing at a big gospel concert in a huge arena, and after the show, I was sitting at my merchandise table with my friend from the orphan's home, Dianne. We watched as an older man walked toward us. We both knew immediately who it was.

The man meekly said, "Hello girls. Do you know who I am?"

We both stammered, "Yes, we know who you are."

The man started to cry. It was Brother Etheredge, our pastor from the orphan's home. He was a man who we had very unkind memories of. He said, "I want to ask your forgiveness for the things that I did, and for the way I treated you and all the others."

We just sat there, stunned, as he went on: "Please forgive me. There's no way I could ever get to see all the kids who were in the orphan's home. But I have come to tell you that I am so sorry. I am a different man today. I have been baptized in the Holy Spirit."

Standing behind him were several matrons from the orphanage. They were now very old, and they also came up to us and asked our forgiveness. We all just cried and hugged, and it was so sweet.

I was asked to perform at a church in Arkansas, and a thunderstorm rolled in right when I was getting ready to start. As I began singing my first song, there was a big lightning flash and a crack of thunder right on top of us. All the lights went out, and my mic and all the speakers went out with them.

My manager went out to the RV and ran an extension cord from the motorhome generator. We were able to power our little sound system, and I did my entire show in the dark! They held flashlights so that people could see me. The lights never came back on, but the service went on! They must have liked it, because they asked me to come back a couple years later.

I am not a pastor. I am a witness. I am a witness for the Lord, and for his love, merciful grace and merciful power. God had a plan for my life. I know that God wanted to use me to help people who were hurting, and to help people who had to go through the same things that I did.

Jesus said, "If you confess me before men, I will confess you before my Father in Heaven." That's what I do. That's what I chose to do with my life. I am a confessor. I run around the world and I confess that Jesus is real. I confess that he changed my life.

If your faith is strong enough, oftentimes the Lord will give you a surprising challenge. My challenge came when God told me to take my favorite grandmother (I say that very sarcastically) to Bethlehem!

So that's exactly what I did. I took Claudine with our church group to Bethlehem. I thought, if she can't change her life here, then she can't change it anywhere. And sure enough, it was there, on Christmas Day, that she gave her heart to Jesus. She had been on our bus with Brother Howard, and when I came aboard, Brother Howard said, "Louise, Claudine has something she wants to tell you."

I just cried and cried when she told me that she had given her heart to Jesus. I couldn't believe it. She instantly became so sweet and so kind, and she told me how much she loved me. I could see and feel Jesus go into her. She really changed, and she started going to church with me. Everything was wonderful.

My pastor, Brother Howard, is the one who helped bring Claudine to the Lord. But Brother Howard died on June 19, 1978, about five years after that trip. And for some reason, after his death, Claudine went back to how she had been all her life. The sweet, loving person she had become after she'd gotten saved now went away, and she went back to the mean person she had been. She and my mother lived in a duplex together, and they spent the rest of their lives fighting with each other.

When I look back on everything now, I think that in the depths of her heart, Claudine wanted to be a nice person. But she had such a hateful spirit, and I know that was because she was so abused as a child. She was terribly abused.

Near the end of her life, Claudine was in a nursing home. I took my kids to see her, and she cussed me out in front of my boys. Then she started cursing at them.

I sent them out into the hallway and I told her, "Don't you ever speak to my children like that again!"

I didn't have to worry about that, because she got so angry that she never spoke to me again. The last words she said to me were cuss words. I don't think Claudine ever found any true peace. At least not while she was alive.

As for me... thank God, I am insanely saved! When I speak in a church, or I meet someone somewhere, I don't want them to just say, "I saw Lulu from Hee Haw." That's great, but I really want them to say, "I saw Lulu, and I saw Jesus in Lulu."

When we were out on the road, Dianne was very protective of me. She didn't want anyone taking advantage of me. Quite often, a church will take up a love offering for any performer that they've brought in. One time, we were in a huge church in Denver, and we watched as they passed buckets around, and the people just filled them up with money.

But at the end of the night, the minister gave us an envelope that had $150 in it. Dianne was furious. She took the pastor aside, and said, "What you have just done is not right, and we will not leave here until you make it right." Miraculously, the minister found a whole bunch of money that just appeared out of nowhere! Hopefully, thanks to Dianne's boldness, that minister will not try to keep an offering that's meant to bless the life of someone else.

During the years when I was constantly on the road, speaking and singing in churches, I saw God do things that were just phenomenal. We had people get healed. I saw a man who had been blind since birth regain his sight. I met so many people who needed some happiness and hope. They found that happiness and hope through my music.

I've also had my share of lighthearted moments during my travels. One of the funniest came when I was on tour with Kelly Willard and Rhonda Hanson. They are both great gospel singers. We were in the middle of a concert at a church in Downsville, Louisiana, singing the song "Sweet Hour of Prayer". It has a line, which goes: "In seasons of distress and grief, my soul has often found relief..."

But Rhonda had always sang the song with the word "heart" in place of "soul". Before the concert, Kelly and I told her that she needed to use the word "soul" like we did. We did the song acapella, with no music, and it was gorgeous. But when we got to that line, Rhonda started to say "heart", then she caught herself, and it came out as "h...ole". She sang, "My hole has often found relief"!

I started immediately thinking of a Preparation H commercial! I got so tickled. I tried to hold in my laughter until we'd finished the song, but the more I held it in, the more my body started to shake! Rhonda reached over and pinched me to try to get me to stop, and then Kelly asked, "What are y'all laughin' at?" right in the middle of the song! The congregation just stared at us. They looked like deer in the headlights. Then they started laughing at us laughing. When we explained everything to them, the entire audience was in tears, they were laughing so hard. It was so funny.

Kelly, Rhonda and I knew we had to retire that song. After that day, there was no way we could get through "Sweet Hour of Prayer" without laughing about Rhonda's hole!

In addition to churches, I also shared my music and testimony at women's conferences. I did one women's conference, and the men who happened to be there enjoyed it so much that they invited me to come back the next year for their men's conference. It turned out great, and I enjoyed it so much.

I had a friend named Mary Ann Brown, who went to the Beverly Hills Baptist in Dallas, where I got saved. Mary Ann was a profit. She HA would stand over someone and prophesy, and it would come out in rhymes, so fast that there was no way she could have made it up. The Lord just gave it to her.

Mary Ann came to my house one night, and asked if she could wash my feet. While she did, she told me that God was going to use me, and that I was going to have an "End Time Ministry." That scared me to death.

Three decades later, as I was in the middle of writing this book, I was doing a show at a church in Minnesota. As I met with people afterward, a woman came up to me, and she just wept and wept. She said, "Lulu, the Lord wants me to tell you that you are an 'End Time Warrior.'" I just fell to pieces, as I remembered what Mary Ann Brown had prophesied 30 years ago.

Over the past year, as I was writing this book, I had no idea what the title should be. So, like always, I took it to the Lord. I prayed that I would find the perfect words. I was not surprised when I found them... in church.

In early 2018, as I sang at an event, I told the crowd that I was working on my book. A little lady came up to me afterward and said, "Lulu, I've got your book title. It should be 'This Is My Story, This Is My Song.'"

You can turn back to the front cover to see what we ended up naming the book. I love it when God shows up around me!

Over the years, I have received many letters from people who have written the words, "You changed my life". I was so grateful for that, but I would always tell them, "No, it wasn't me. It was all the Lord."

I believe with my whole heart that I was born to do what I do. My passion is to get souls for Jesus. While the Hee Haw show was a huge vehicle for me, I truly believe that I was born to get souls for the Lord. And I get them anywhere I can!

Sometimes, I even get them at Walmart! I love Walmart. I call myself the Walmart Queen. I love to sit and talk to people there. I talk to them to brighten my own day, and also to brighten theirs. Many times, people will be surprised when I say "Good morning! How are you doing?" as I'm shopping. You would be surprised at how many people there are who never have anyone say hello to them. If you walk by someone in the parking lot and tell them, "God loves you.

Have a wonderful day," you are doing something important for the Lord.

There are so many lonely people in the world, many right in your community, and YOU have the power to brighten their day just by giving them a smile and a kind word. And you will end up getting as much, or more from it, than they do.

I can't tell you what an incredible feeling it is to be at a church service and see a hundred, or two hundred, people come forward to give their lives to Jesus. But I am just as thrilled to be able to help bring just one person to the Lord.

One of my friends was with a friend who was dying in the hospital. She called me and said, "Lulu, he doesn't know the Lord. He probably doesn't even have ten minutes."

I said, "Put him on the phone."

The first thing he said was, "Lulu, I'm scared. I don't know the Lord." I talked to him, and he ended up saying the sinner's prayer there on the phone with me. He gave his heart to Jesus, and he died just a few minutes later. I was so touched that the Lord had used me to bring that man to him.

More than ten years ago, I met a very special couple during one of my concerts. I was at a church in Little Rock, Arkansas, and a man and his wife were sitting in the front row. I kept looking at them as I sang, and I felt like I knew them, even though we had never met before. Their names were Jackie and Lauretta Tedford, and I met them for the first time after my show. The Lord just bonded us immediately, and we became best friends.

I was still at a place in my life where I did not like being touched. I was uncomfortable whenever someone touched me. It took many years for me to get to a point where I would let someone hug or touch me. But Lauretta was the one that showed me how to hug. She could feel me trying to pull away, and she would just pull me closer and hold me tighter. She taught me how to be held.

Lauretta was tall and regal. She was smart, and had skin like porcelain. She was the epitome of class. She was a sister that anyone would want, and our spirits just bonded. Lauretta taught me how to accept love, and how to be loved. She had a heart that just drew people to her. She really changed my life.

When Lauretta and Jackie celebrated their 50th wedding anniversary, I sang at their celebration. Lauretta died in October of 2015, but even after her death, I have stayed close with Jackie. He lives in Arkansas, but he comes to Nashville a couple of times a year to visit, and he is always in the front row any time I am within driving distance of where he lives.

In addition to churches, I also started doing a prison ministry. I'd always wanted to go inside the prisons to see what it was like, and what I had just missed out on! I knew that it was only by the grace of God that I was going into the prisons as a visitor, and not as an inmate.

One of the first prisons I visited was in Texas. It just happened to be where I would have been sent if I had been convicted of the drug charges I was arrested for, a few years earlier. After the service, one of the female inmates came up and said, "Don't worry, Lulu. If you wind up in here, we'll take care of you and make sure no one ever hurts you."

I will never forget our visit to the prison in Huntsville. It was such an incredible experience. It was an experience for everyone, for the inmates, for the guards, and for us. When we first went in, I saw a gymnasium full of the most hardened women. They all looked so mean. We looked at each other and said, "What are we doing here?" Then we saw the guards. They looked worse than the inmates!

I sang, and then Dianne and I sang together. We had also brought along Pastor Larry Lea to sing a song, and then I gave my testimony. I got their attention right off the bat, when I said, "I'm supposed to be in here with you."

At the end of my talk, I said, "If any of you want to reach out to the Lord and really let him touch your heart, just come on down here, and we will pray for you." And every one of those women got up and just ran toward the stage! They were knocking the chairs over to get there. It was so moving that the guards started hugging the prisoners! It was unbelievable.

The chaplain over all of the prisons in the state was a tremendous Christian. He was there that day too, and he told me, "I have to let you know that I have never, ever seen this before." That day was the start of a religious revival in the Huntsville prisons, with both the women's and men's prison.

When I went to the men's prison in Huntsville, there was not enough room for all the inmates who wanted to be at the service. Those that couldn't get in sat in the windows, and I could hear them singing the hymns with us. God had gotten them ready before I'd ever got there.

I recently went to a women's prison in Missouri. There were 800 women in the audience, and we had so many of them give their hearts to Jesus. Over the years, I've had a few men and women outside come up and say to me that they had been inmates when I came to share my testimony in their prison.

But my most life-changing prison experience came at the Leavenworth, Kansas penitentiary. After I gave my testimony, an inmate came up to me and said, "My name is Gary. You are a beautiful woman."

I said, "Gary, you are a lyin' dog!"

Gary was good-looking, and he said he was a Christian. After we talked a little, he asked if he could write me a letter. I said, "Sure you can!"

And we ended up writing many letters back and forth.

Gary had grown up in Idaho. He'd been adopted by a father who told him, "I don't care a thing about you. I adopted you so I won't have to go to war." His great new "dad" went on to tell him, "You ain't never gonna amount to nothin'."

That lack of love and support helped lead Gary to life of trouble. He was in trouble all the time. He got arrested for writing bad checks, and then he got arrested again for stealing a car.

Gary had been sentenced to nine years in prison for motor vehicle theft. He served six of those years before he was released, but while he was behind bars, he wrote me the most lovely, wonderful, beautiful letters. We wrote back and forth for a year, and Gary's letters were poetic. He talked about his desire to love me, and his desire to give me the life of my dreams. He said everything that a lonely fat girl would want to hear. I had never had anyone talk to me like he did in his letters, and I went for it, hook, line and sinker. I wouldn't find out until much later, and much too late, that it was his cellmate who had been writing the letters for him! I didn't find that out until I had married Gary!

A year after our pen pal romance began, Gary was released from prison. We started dating immediately, and we were married just three months after his release. On my wedding day, July 5, 1975, I knew that I was not really in love with Gary. I just didn't want to be alone anymore. My maid of honor, Virginia Widner, was with me as I was getting ready.

I said, "Let's get out of here. Let's run out the back door!"

But Virginia said, "You can't! There's 400 people out there." So I went through with the wedding.

Our ceremony was held at Beverly Hills Baptist Church. The church pastor, Howard Conatser, performed the ceremony, while my son Damon served as ring bearer. I also invited my grandmother Claudine to the wedding. I wanted to show her that I had forgiven her for the hateful words she had used toward me for so many years.

Gary's last name was Toman, so I went from Lulu Roman to Lulu Toman. We spent our honeymoon in the Lake of the Ozarks, but the honeymoon didn't last long! From the minute I married him, it was hell. Gary was very nice. He was a sweet man... until he lost his temper. He loved to drink. He loved to go to bars, and I didn't. I told him I wasn't going with him to any bar.

We were never in love with each other. We were in lust. While we were married two and a half years, I don't think he was in the house three months. He took a job as an over the road truck driver. And while he was on the road, he began seeing other women. He was not through sowing his wild oats.

On October 12, 1976, I filed for divorce. The next day, Gary came begging for my forgiveness, and begging me to give him another chance. He promised he would be a different man. I don't think I ever truly believed him, but I wanted to be sure I had done everything I could to make my marriage work. So I took him back.

For the next year, I put up with the same stuff... from the same, unchanged Gary. I filed for divorce again on December 29, 1977, and it became final two months later. During the last year of our marriage, Gary was hardly ever home. But he did stay around long enough to get me pregnant.

My son Damon was four and half years old when I got the news that I was carrying my second child. I completely freaked out. I met with my pastor, Brother Howard. Pastor Howard was the only person who was like a father to me. I told him that I didn't want to have the baby.

He took my hands, and said, "Honey, listen to me. You love this baby, but you don't want to go through the same experience you did with your first child birth, and you are afraid of that."

That was all true. I was scared to death that they were going to cut me to pieces again.

Brother Howard calmed my fears and on June 3, 1976, at 5:33 p.m., when I first laid my eyes on Justin Collin Roman, I knew I had made the right decision. But like my first son Damon, my second baby also had to fight for his life, from the moment he was born.

Fluid was filling up Justin's right lung. He was very jaundiced, and he was breathing 150 times a minute. He spent the first five days of his life in the intensive care unit. But, after lots of prayers were sent up by many people, Justin was well enough to come home. And he very quickly turned into a gorgeous baby, with light blonde hair and big, bright blue eyes. He was the cutest little pumpkin you ever saw.

Just after Justin was born, I built my dream house in DeSoto, Texas. It was a 6,000 square foot house, and it was just wonderful. In our living room was a baby grand piano, and in our driveway was a new Lincoln Continental. Yes, life was good. That fat girl on Hee Haw had officially made it!

I had always loved swimming pools, so I put a beautiful, 40 foot pool in my back yard. When Damon was three years old, and Justin was just a tiny baby, I taught them both to swim. I loved to be in the water, and they both loved our pool as much as I did.

On May 3, 1979, a tornado tore through our neighborhood. It shattered the back glass window of my Lincoln, blew down our fence, damaged our roof, and tore up a lot of our swimming pool equipment. But when the storm had passed, I thanked the Lord that we were all safe.

One day, when Justin was about three, we were swimming in the pool when he told me he had to go to the bathroom. So he got out and ran toward the house. I had just made a chocolate cake, and I remembered then that it was on the counter. As he ran in, I yelled, "Don't you touch that cake!"

After a few minutes, I went to check on him, and I found him standing in the kitchen. He had chocolate smeared all over his face, in his hair, and all over his hands. He had it on his bathing suit, and even on his legs. He had chocolate everywhere!

I yelled, "Justin, I told you not to get in that cake!"

He looked up and said, "I didn't, mommy."

I grabbed him by the arm and took him to the bathroom, where I had huge mirrors that covered the entire wall. I stood Justin up on the counter, and when he saw that chocolate all over him, he started screaming! It was so funny, all I could do was laugh.

But I wasn't laughing a couple years later, when Justin started getting into trouble at school. When he was in kindergarten, I was called to the school after he had punched a teacher in the nose. Justin was a little booger, who always worried me. He would lie, cheat and steal. He was very mischievous. When he was in the fourth grade, I got him a chemistry set, and he nearly burned the house down. He'd put all the chemicals together and started a fire in his room.

By the time he got to the fifth grade, he was in trouble all the time. But one of the teachers gave him a series of IQ tests, and he scored a 160! The teacher said, "No wonder he gets in trouble. He's a fifth grader with a 160 IQ. He must be totally bored!"

So they moved him up a grade, and the more he had to study, the less trouble he got into.

Justin was so smart. They had a competition for all the schools in the Fort Worth, Texas area, and out of all the tens of thousands of students there, my son got the silver medal for math, and the bronze medal for science. I've still got those medals today. Justin was the kind of kid that any mom and dad would love to have.

My children loved me. I am so thankful for that, and every day I told both my little boys that I loved them. I wanted to be the best mom that I could possibly be to my two children. I always told them how precious they were to me, and how valuable they were. No one had ever told me that. I grew up thinking I was worthless. I was told that I was stupid and lazy, and I wanted to make sure my boys knew that they were loved, they were smart, and they could do anything they wanted to in life.

When I started on Hee Haw, I didn't have any kids, but my two sons grew up on the Hee Haw set. All of the cast got to watch my boys grow up, and everyone loved my boys. They treated them so great. Grandpa Jones really loved my boys, and they loved him. Gordie Tapp came to me once and said, "Lulu, when we started this show, I would have bet you $10 million dollars that you would have never had children. But I am so proud of you. You have raised those sons so well. They are so nice and smart."

I was only married to Justin's father Gary for a very short time, and they didn't really get to know each other until Justin was a grown man. Gary and I had no contact with each other for more than two decades, and by the time Justin decided he wanted to see him, I had no idea of how to reach Gary. I didn't even know which state he lived in. But with the help of a private investigator, we finally located him in late 1998. I was so happy to find that Gary had remarried to a lovely Christian woman, and that they had a wonderful family.

Over the next few years, Justin became close to his father. They loved each other very much. God also allowed me to have a warm relationship with Gary and his wife, Bobbie. When Justin graduated from the University of Tennessee at Martin on August 1, 1999, for the first time in his life, both his mother and father were there to support and celebrate him.

I never even married Damon's dad. But I always told my sons, "You will never hear me say anything bad about your daddy." All I'd ever wanted in my life was a daddy, so I wasn't about to say anything hateful about the dads my sons had.

But I always told my sons the truth, if they ever asked me anything about their fathers. I told them the truth, whether it was good or bad. My sons didn't get much time with their fathers during their childhood years, but when they grew up, they both ended up having very good relationships with their dads.

FROM MY DREAM LOVER TO A NIGHTMARE

After Hee Haw was cancelled, I devoted more time to my recording career. But I quickly found that hit records and big sellers were hard to come by. It seemed that the Country Music world didn't want me because I was too Gospel, and the Gospel music world didn't want me because I was too Country. So I just kind of wandered around lost, looking for a place that wanted me. I knew that "the people", my fans, wanted me. They were always there for me.

But if getting a hit song was tough... finding a good man was almost impossible!

Up to this point in my life, I hadn't had much luck with men. It seemed that I was always making the wrong choices when it came to men. Little did I know that I was about to make the all-time worst choice of my life.

During my school years, one of the hit songs on the radio was "Dream Lover" by Bobby Darin. As we listened to that song, all of us girls would sit around and talk about our dream lover. I told them that my dream man would be tall, with dark, curly hair, a mustache, and he would wear a white uniform. Be careful what you dream, girls!

My dear friend Molly was working as a hairstylist at Neiman Marcus. One day, she told me that she worked with a man who was also a hairstylist. She explained that he was a huge fan of mine, and had asked her to introduce him to me. His name was Woody Smith.

Molly asked if she could bring him by my house the following week, and I agreed. When I opened the door, there stood my "dream lover". He was exactly the man I had pictured in my mind back when I was just a teenager! Woody was tall and slender, with dark, curly hair, and a mustache. While he wasn't wearing a white uniform like I had dreamed, he was wearing a white sweater, and white pants with white shoes.

I just stood there looking at him. When I finally asked him to come in, he met my two little boys. Woody told them that, when he wasn't doing hair, he rode horses, and cleaned out the horse barns and stables.

After our initial meeting, Woody and I made a date for the upcoming weekend. He said he'd be there Saturday at 7:00. But when 7:00 came, he didn't. I watched the clock pass 8:00, and then 9:00… and at 10:00, I finally went to bed. I couldn't believe that he didn't show up. I was heartbroken.

The next day, at 2:00 in the afternoon, the phone rang. It was Woody, who said he wanted to come in person to apologize. I reluctantly agreed. I don't remember what his excuse was, but he kept insisting that he was so sorry. So I forgave him, and we set another date, and he did show up for that one. And we really hit it off.

Before I knew it, I was married to a cowboy! On October 8, 1979, Woody and I were married at the Calvary Baptist Church in Cleburne, Texas. I wrote in my diary, "He really loves me!"

Woody loved wearing cowboy hats, boots and jeans, and I didn't mind a bit. He was such a good-lookin' man, I'd have let him wear anything he wanted! Though I was a bit disappointed when I found out that the beautiful, curly hair I had loved when we first met was really a fabulous hairpiece! Since he was a hairdresser, he could fix it to where no one could ever tell that he wore a rug.

Woody and I had a pretty good marriage for a couple of years. It was really good. Our sex life was pretty good. In the beginning of our marriage, we had some really great moments. We would slow dance in the living room, and he could sweep me off my feet.

Woody wanted a baby. He wanted to be a father, and he was the absolute perfect father to my son Justin. Justin was just two years old at the time, and Woody adored him. He treated Justin like he was his own baby boy. Woody adopted Justin and Damon on February 13, 1980, and they took Woody's last name of Smith.

I once took a road trip with Woody and his mother Marcelle, and it was a trip that I will never forget. Marcelle lived in Cleburne, Texas, about an hour from our house in Desoto, and she would come and stay with us to help take care of the boys. One day, she had her best friend Juanita come along with her. When we got back home, we all loaded up in the car to drive them back to Cleburne.

I was in the front seat, and my husband was driving. The back seat was full, with our two boys, and Marcelle and Juanita. There was a stretch of road between Cleburne and Desoto where there was nothing for about 30 minutes. There were no gas stations, no restaurants… no place at all to stop.

Right when we got in the middle of that stretch, Juanita told my husband, "Woody, you need to stop at a gas station."

He said, "There ain't a station for quite a while."

A couple minutes later, she says, "Woody, you have to find a gas station! I have to go to the bathroom!"

Again, he said, "There is no gas station for miles!"

After a minute, she quietly said, "I think I'm getting diarrhea." My husband and I just looked at each other. A minute later, she yelled, "Stop the damn car!"

Woody quickly pulled over and got the car stopped, right next to a big rock ravine. There was a little hill just a couple steps off the road. The moment the car stopped, Juanita threw open her door. Before she was even all the way out of the car, she started pulling her pants down. My son Justin screamed, "Oh no!"

We could all see that she was starting to poop before she was out of the car. There was poop all over the seat! As she took her first step out, she slipped and fell down the little hill. She was pooping as she was falling! That ravine was covered with tiny pebbles and rocks, and when she tried to get up, she tripped over her pants and fell again, right in her own s--t! And then she rolled over!

When Juanita got up, she had poop in her hair, on her face, and one side of her was covered with rocks and poop. She was screaming and cussing, and all of us were laughing our heads off! We didn't even have a Kleenex tissue in the car. We had nothing, no towel, nothing that she could use. So she started trying to wipe it all off with her hands!

My boys in the back seat were screaming! Her entire right side, from her head to toe, had been covered with rocks and poop. She scraped off as much as she could and got back into the car. And…what's that smell?! It smelled so bad. She had s--t all down her face. The rest of us could not stop laughing, and the more we laughed, the madder she got. The kids in the back were gagging. We put all four windows down, but everyone was holding their noses. Yes, it was a road trip I'll never forget.

If only we could have laughed so hard every day. But soon, I would be finding very little humor in my marriage. One of the first negatives, and it really wasn't horrible, came when Woody insisted on me using his last name. So, even though the world knew me as Lulu Roman, Woody made me add Smith to it. So, on all of my appearances, I was billed as Lulu Roman Smith. I was happy that he was so proud that I was his wife. He wanted everyone to know that we were married. But the added name made things a little confusing for some of my fans and concert bookers.

Woody was a good man, and he tried very hard. But he was screwed up. His father was rich, a millionaire, but he was also a sick man. He had abused his kids so bad. One Christmas, Woody's dad got so mad at his kids that he locked them all inside a closet for the entire day. They didn't get to open their gifts, or even have Christmas dinner. That kind of childhood led to some bad things for Woody.

Woody drank from sunup to sundown. He drank vodka. I could smell it in his coffee. I really think it was Woody's relationship with his own father that drove him to alcohol. His father was a drunk, and I think his abuse caused Woody to start drinking at a very early age.

While Woody was just the best dad he could be for Justin, I noticed that his relationship with Damon was different. I would soon find out why. Woody was bisexual. I called him tri-sexual, because he would try anything. He did not act like he was gay, not at all. You couldn't tell it at all. He was a macho cowboy.

One day, Damon, Justin and I had just come in from the pool. I was in my room when Damon came in. Oprah was on TV, and the subject was pedophiles. They were talking about men touching boys. Damon looked at me, and said very quietly, "Mommy, that's what daddy did to me."

I asked him what he said, and he repeated the same thing. I said, "Hold on baby. Mommy has to go to the bathroom. I'll be right back."

I went into the bathroom and sat on my beautiful garden tub and I prayed, "OK God… you have to help me with this one. If you don't, I'm gonna get my gun and I'm going to kill a son of a b----!" But at that moment, I could very plainly hear the Lord saying, "Do not make your children orphans like you were." I knew then that if I would have killed my husband, he would be dead, I would be in prison and my two boys would not have any parents.

The whole time Woody had been treating my son Justin so wonderfully, he was abusing my other son Damon. I didn't know anything about it. All of that had also hurt the relationship between Damon and Justin. I didn't shoot and kill Woody that day. But I sure did have him arrested. He went before the judge, and was sentenced to counseling and classes for a couple years. I divorced him. We had been married for nine years.

If you've read my book this far, you know that I have done some stupid things in my life. I have made some horrible choices. Most of the heartache I have suffered is because of poor decisions I've made. But I am about to share with you the dumbest and most unbelievable decision I have ever made! You won't believe it when you read it. If you think you've done some dumb things in your life... you are about to be topped!

We didn't see Woody for a couple of years. But I had an event in Cleburne, Texas, where Woody was from, and while I was there, he dropped in on us. He brought a very heartfelt apology letter that he had written. Woody was a mastermind at getting back to where he wanted to be, and I somehow, someway, let him back into our lives. And, get ready for it... before long, we got married a second time!! How stupid can one woman be?!

Woody and I were remarried on February 14, 1988. Valentine's Day! I thought that was so romantic. My son Damon did not. Damon was very hurt, and very upset with me for a long time. Who could blame him? Here he was, 11 years old, and his mom is letting the man who had sexually abused him back into our home.

Woody told us he was now a Godly man, and that he wanted to have a Godly family. My boys wanted that, too. But I don't think I really trusted him again. I never let him be alone with either of my sons.

The "new" Woody was also lazy. He wouldn't work. He wouldn't help pay the rent. He wouldn't take care of the kids. All he wanted to do was lay around and get drunk. We stayed married for less than two years. During that time, I lost my dream home. I just couldn't afford it, especially with a husband who wouldn't get a job. We moved into an apartment, and I traded in my new Lincoln Continental for a used car. Then I filed for bankruptcy.

All the material possessions I had worked so hard for were gone, almost overnight. So what did I do? I sang. Every day, I sang, "I'd rather have Jesus than anything…"

I sang that song as I moved from Texas to Nashville. I was 42 years old. I must admit that I had lived a pretty eventful 42 years!

Somebody told me I should write a book. I responded, "Maybe in 30 years or so!"

My ex-husband Woody died ten years after I moved to Nashville. I didn't even know it until many years after his death. No one ever let me know. I didn't cry when I found out. I never shed a tear. But I was upset when I found out how he had died. They said that he'd died in his sleep after having a heart attack. He never woke up. Yes, I was upset, because I had wanted him to suffer a very painful death. But I did get a big laugh when I heard that his wife had him cremated. Then one night, she got drunk and poured all his ashes in the rosebushes in their backyard. I got to thinking about Woody, scattered in the bushes, and when it rained hard, I knew he was running down the street and he probably ended up in a dirty alley, where he belonged!

Before I close the chapter on Woody, I want to say one more thing, and I ask that you use it in your own life. Throughout my life, I have learned that you have to choose to be a forgiver. I had to choose to forgive the family that threw me away.

I was very, very angry at my mother and father for a long time. I was also angry at God. When no parent ever chose to take me out of that orphanage, I thought that God had dumped me. Of course, now I know that God didn't dump me. He chose me!

But because of all of the anger I felt, I went on to make every kind of wrong choice that you can make in your life. So I also had to choose to forgive myself for all of the stupid choices I had made.

Yes, I had to forgive Woody for what he did to my son and to our family. That's easier said than done, believe me. But when you choose to forgive, that person who had wounded you so deeply no longer defines who you are. And you can allow the blood of Jesus to define who you are. That is freedom. That gives you peace of mind that nothing else can give you... nothing but the blood of Jesus.

A TV STAR IS BORN

During the more than 20 years that I was on Hee Haw, I also enjoyed being a guest star on quite a few other TV shows and movies.

I did a movie called "Corky" in 1972. Robert Blake was the main star. It was a few years before he became Baretta on TV. He played an angry race car driver in "Corky", and I played a gum-smacking waitress in a beer joint. I only had two or three lines.

In 1983, I was on "The Love Boat". It was a country music episode. Kenny Price and I fell in love with each other, and ate our way across the ship. It was very fun. Minnie Pearl and Tanya Tucker were also on. Everyone on the show was extremely nice to me. But we didn't go on a real cruise. It was all filmed on a set in Hollywood!

I filmed the show "City Confidential" in 1998. It was an episode about the murder of Hee Haw and Opry star Stringbean. I was part of the show, and Roy Clark, Grandpa Jones and Bill Anderson were also in it.

I did an episode of "Touched by an Angel" in 2001. In that show, I was part of a gospel music-singing family. Of course, I could relate to that... but when I read the script, I found out that our bus went over a cliff and we all died! It was just a small, non-speaking role.

I still enjoy acting. I'd love to do more movies or TV shows. I like television better, because it is much faster. I never ever dreamed for a second that I would become a "celebrity". I still can't use that word when I talk about myself. It just doesn't fit. I am an actress. I'm a singer, and I am a comedian. But I have a hard time seeing myself as a celebrity or star. I don't look at anyone else as a "star", or as any better than another person, even if someone has had great achievements. We are all God's creatures.

When Hee Haw was at its peak of popularity, we took a live version of the show to both Branson, Missouri and to Las Vegas. A few years later, Roy Clark would become one of the kings of Branson, when he opened his own theater. Both Roy and Buck Owens played the big casinos and hotels in Las Vegas for a number of years. I always enjoyed playing in Vegas or Branson with any of my Hee Haw friends.

I also did a one-woman show in Branson for a couple years. It was so much fun. We had packed houses every night. It was one of the best times of my life and career. It let me know that I had the ability to entertain people. I could do an entire show just by myself, and people would love it.

A LITTLER LULU

Women do not like to talk about their age, or about any "work they have had done". You almost never hear a TV or music "star" give up any secrets about things they have had done to improve their appearance. All those perfect people were just born like that... totally natural. Yeah right!

But I figure if I'm going to write my autography, I might as well tell the whole truth, and nothing but the truth. If I don't, then what's the point? So get ready Lulu fans... you're about to find out some things NOBODY has ever known!

You might have noticed, but I was once a little overweight. Ha! At my heaviest, I weighed almost 400 pounds. I am 5'6" tall. So maybe I really wasn't overweight... I was really 4 feet too short! I have had a weight problem all my life. I don't remember one day that I wasn't overweight.

I am the sugar queen. I love dark chocolate, and I can eat more sugar than anyone I know, but my blood sugar levels are normal. I guess that's because I started eating a lot of sugar when I was very young. It was always hard for me to lose weight. Even in high school, I weighed at least 250. I tried everything I could, and I couldn't lose weight. I've been on every diet in the world, but they just didn't work for me.

When I was 61 years old, I was really in trouble. My health was very bad. I started using a scooter to get around. I couldn't walk, and my back was in horrible shape. I couldn't travel. I couldn't stand up. I couldn't breathe. I had asthma and high blood pressure. I knew I had to make a change to save my health and save my life.

In 2003, I had lap band surgery. That's where they put a band around the top of your tummy and it restricts your intake of food. I kind of felt like I was cheating, but I got over that when the weight started to fall off! I lost 80 pounds in no time.

But I had to have the lap band removed a year later, when I became allergic to it. I got very sick when my body rejected it, and I had to have it taken off.

I decided to try a second lap band surgery in 2007, and that decision almost turned out to be a fatal one. I was so intent on losing the weight that I said, "Even if it kills me, I'm going to keep this lap band in." And it almost did kill me.

I was so thrilled with all the weight I was losing… 10 or 15 pounds a week! On top of the 80 pounds I'd lost a couple years earlier, I lost another 130! But I could also feel that something wasn't right. I figured that my body was rejecting the lap band again. But I didn't want to go through another surgery to have it removed, and I almost died.

Another strike against my health was my hatred of water. I always hated water, and I still don't drink water, even today. But I almost stopped drinking entirely when I had the lap band, and I got very dehydrated. I had stopped eating, and then I stopped drinking. I got so weak, and my body started shutting down. My whole system was dying.

I was at a show in Texas in 2010, and I had to have people help me walk up on stage. I sat down in a chair as soon as I got up there. I was weak and shaking. I tried to act like I had an upset stomach. I had no idea that I had developed an infection inside my stomach.

I went to the hospital immediately after my performance. They had to perform a major surgery to take the band out, and when they opened me up, they found gangrene around that lap band. The surgeon had to clean out all of my insides. It took me a couple years to get over it.

When all of those ordeals were over, I was astonished to learn that I had lost 222 pounds! I went from a size 56-58 to a size 14-16. I still have pants that I used to wear. I can stand with my entire body in one of the pant legs! But I nearly died to do it.

I actually ended up losing too much weight. I got down to 160 pounds. I didn't even look like myself. I don't know who I looked like, but it wasn't Lulu Roman.

I had to return to the hospital, until I started gaining weight. I have enough scar tissue from all those surgeries that now I can't sit down and eat a big meal like everyone else. I have to eat very small meals, but I get hungry again half an hour later.

When I was forced to have the lap band removed permanently, I was terrified that I would gain back all the weight that I had lost. But I prayed, and asked God to help me maintain my weight. I also exercised as much as I could, and I tried to watch what I ate. All of that has helped me to stay on track and keep my weight down. I am now at 215 pounds, and I feel great. I would love to get down to 190 or 195, but I'm not making any big effort to get down more.

But a strange thing happened when I had lost all that weight... it was strange, and kind of sad, too. A lot of people seemed to feel like I wasn't jovial anymore. To a lot of people, I was funnier when I was morbidly obese! Too bad!

I might have had my last lap band surgery, but I was only just beginning to see the inside of the hospital operating room.

When you lose over 200 pounds, all of the fat is gone... but all of that ugly, stretched out excess skin is still hanging on you! To get rid of that, I had a tummy tuck two times. I also had my arms reduced, with the saggy skin all removed. I'd actually had a breast reduction way back in 1992. My huge boobs were destroying my back, and I had another breast reduction in 2009.

NOW GET READY FOR A MAJOR CONFESSION!

You'll get the scoop before The National Enquirer!

In 2009, I also had a facelift! The surgeon did an amazing job, and I was so thrilled with the result. I have scars on the back of my neck. You can't see them, unless I want to show you. Most people who have cosmetic surgery on their face can't quit. They'll get one procedure, and then they don't stop. They keep going until they look much worse than they ever did. I am not one of those people! I stopped at one, and have no desire to have another. I'll let Mother Nature have her way with me from here on in.

I want to share something that happened as I was coming out of one of my reconstruction surgeries: I was lying in my hospital bed, with my head turned toward the window. I had been resting with my eyes closed, and as I started to open them, I saw a 10 foot being in front of me. He was wearing a long, flowing white robe, with his hands outstretched. Everything was almost iridescent.

I blinked my eyes to get a better look, and as I opened them wider, the figure was gone. But I truly feel that I had seen my angel. I prayed to God many times, and asked him if this was indeed my guardian angel. I also asked him for the name of the angel. As I listened for an answer, I heard "Isaiah." I got my Bible and turned to Isaiah 43, and read of the promise of restoration and protection. I had no doubt that I was being watched over as my body recovered.

And I did recover. I cruised right on through my 60s, headed toward the big 7-0. I had planned to celebrate my 70th birthday fairly quietly, but Kim, my assistant, had different ideas. She told me that a couple of friends had come in from out of town, and they wanted to take me to dinner.

But when I got to what I had thought would be an intimate dinner, I quickly found that Kim had arranged a huge surprise party for me. More than 200 people packed the George Jones Museum to celebrate with me! I walked in, and I could not believe it when everyone screamed "Happy Birthday!" The first person I saw was Randy Travis! Then I saw George Jones' wife Nancy, and Uncle Si from Duck Dynasty! I thought I was gonna have a heart attack right then and there. So many of my friends were there. I was completely surprised. I had no idea it was going to happen.

My 70th birthday was awesome. But the rest of my 70th year went downhill from there! I went through a very hard year. It was hard, both physically and mentally. Little did I know that it would be a total cakewalk, compared to my 71st year. I'll have much more about that in a couple chapters.

But right now, let me get real honest with you. As you get older, your life changes. Not all for the better. As the years go by, you find out that you have to deal with death much more than you ever have. I have had so many friends and family members die in recent years. I count on the Lord to boost my spirit during those tough times.

When you reach your 70s, you also get to see your doctor on a regular basis. One of the first things my doctor always asks me is, "Are you drinking your water?"

And I say, "No! I hate water!" But I do drink water, as long as it's in sweet tea! And I cannot drink carbonated drinks. So I drink a lot of Minute Maid Peach drinks. If you see me singing or speaking in a church, that's what you'll probably see me drinking.

I could still be very busy on the road. I am honored to still get so many requests to perform around the country. I still do a lot. But I can't travel as much as I used to. I've had one knee replacement. People tell you there's nothing to having your knee replaced. Let me tell you that they are lying! You will have murder in your heart for a month after your surgery! Then, when you get almost recovered,

they'll ask you if you want the other knee done. My answer…
NOOOOO!

I've also been diagnosed with arthritis. I have arthritis in my knees, my hips, shoulders, wrists, and my ankles, and the pain in my back never stops. My knees, legs and back can't travel like they once did. But I still do 25 to 40 concerts a year.

Unfortunately, I've gotten to know many of my doctors quite well over the last few years. But in 2008, I actually became a doctor! The North Carolina College of Theology gave me a Doctorate degree in Sacred Music. Yes, you can call me "Dr. Lulu"! I was actually in the line of people who were handed their diploma. I still have my graduation gown from the ceremony. I had sang there every summer for more than ten years. I think "the Reverend Dr. Lulu Roman" has a nice ring to it!

TAMMY AND DOTTIE

I'd like to talk about two very special women, who both shared the love of Jesus and spread the word of God to millions of people. Tammy Faye Bakker and Dottie Rambo were both true blessings to the life of Lulu Roman.

I met Jim and Tammy Faye Bakker back when they lived in a little house in South Carolina. They had just started their ministry. They had moved their ministry into a furniture store, and it just kept growing and growing. I knew them throughout most of my adult life.

I loved both Jim and Tammy dearly, and they loved me. Every big celebration they had, they'd invite me and my family to. They had a big parade, and I rode on a float wearing my Hee Haw overalls. They were always so precious to me. Tammy was the dearest soul. She had the heart of an innocent child.

Jim and Tammy were two kids who really wanted to get people to Jesus. That was their objective. I never saw them misbehave in any way. I never saw anything that told me they were hungry for money. I will forevermore stand next to them. Jim and Tammy were not what the world made them out to be. Jim was not a thief. He wasn't, and Tammy was not either. Tammy was terribly abused by the world.

Tammy was the sweetest person you would ever meet, and you never told her that you liked what she had on, because she would give it to you right there! She would take off her jewelry, her shoes, she'd clean out her purse and give it to you, if you mentioned how nice it was.

I had an 8 karat CZ diamond ring, which was heart-shaped and was very expensive. And when Tammy saw me wear it on her show, she insisted that I come with her to her apartment above their TV studio. When I got there, she went to her safe and got out a pair of heart-shaped diamond ear rings and put them in my hand.

I said, "Tammy, I can't take these."

"You will hurt my heart if you don't," she replied.

So I yelled, "Mine!"

Jim and Tammy were so sweet. But they had some terrible people who got into their organization, and those people made up stories about them. There were people who had moved in and gained Jim's confidence, and they just took over. It all ended up with Jim being sent to prison. Jim and Tammy were so young and innocent when they started. They trusted the wrong people. They gave their ministry to people who ended up destroying it, and destroying them.

Tammy's heart was so big. If she saw a dog that didn't have a home, she'd try to save it. She had the sweetest heart. I saw her take blouses and sweaters that she loved and give them to people who needed clothes.

I knew that Tammy Faye was beginning to lose her battle with cancer. Just before Tammy died, the Lord told me to go see her. I walked in, and just got up in the bed with her. I gathered her up in my arms and just rocked her. As I held her, I told her how beautiful Jesus thought she was.

I whispered, "The Lord wants me to tell you something. He loves you so much. You are still his child, and he is ready to receive you." She knew it was God talking to her. It wasn't just words that I was saying. After a minute, Tammy could just barely whisper, as she said, "There is something I want you to have. I want you to go into my closet and it's on the top shelf."

The Hee Haw cast loved my sons! They made Grandpa look tall

*Jon Hager with
Damon*

Buck and my son Damon

Damon enjoys a Coke and a smile from Cathy Baker.

Archie Campbell and Damon

George Lindsey and Damon

Gaylard Sartain and Damon

Always ready with a smile for the camera

Backstage at the Opry with Minnie Pearl

Thank you so much Linda!

Hope you enjoy Lulu's book.

Scotland England England Media

Kenny Price and I arrive in Hollywood, April 1982

Kenny Price and I film a scene for The Love Boat

My husband Woody, me, Gavin MacLeod, Kenny Price

A behind the scenes photo while we filmed Love Boat

Filming the Hee Haw Honey show

My husband Woody, Kathy Lee Gifford, Lulu

Visiting with Jon Hager

The photographer said, "Look serious."

Sam Lovullo, the man who never gave up on me

Linda Thompson, Lulu, Sam Lovullo, Misty Rowe

Buck Owens and Charley Pride

Visiting Glen Campbell backstage

I loved Tammy Wynette. Photo courtesy Judy Mock

With the amazing Dottie West

On the PTL Club with Jim and Tammy Faye Bakker

My last photo with Tammy Faye Bakker, just before she passed away.

With The Whites

On the set with my dear friend Sharon White

Singing **Two More Hands** *with Ricky Skaggs and Sharon White*

Promo Photo

My son Justin visits me in the recording studio.

My dear friend Dianne. She stills prays for me each day.

With Gunilla Hutton

Damon, Justin, Justin's father Gary and assorted family members

Celebrating birthday with Jeff Smith

Jailhouse Rock. Linda, Misty, Cathy, me and our hairstlist Gwen Anken Bauer

Celebrating Thanksgiving with Grandpa Jones' family

A kiss from Gaylard Sartain

Filming Touched by an Angel with Mark Lowry, Rue McClanahan and David Phelps

*With actress
Delta Burke*

My dear friend Norman Holland. No one believed in me like he did

Riding in style in the back of a limo with Norman Holland

I was always so proud of my two boys

Family portraits with my sons

With Justin and our puppy Sissy

Before and After my huge weight loss

Molly Madely, one of my life long friends

A reunion with Roni Stoneman , Roy Clark and Gordie Tapp

Russ Taff and I celebrate our hit King of Who I Am

Lily Tomlin made it big on Laugh In. That show led to Hee Haw

Visiting with Lily Tomlin and Dottie Rambo

Dottie Rambo. One of the greatest people I ever met

The Golden Girls of Gospel. Lulu, Dottie Rambo, Naomi Sego

Showing off my North Carolina College of Theology Doctorate degree in Sacred Music

The Doctor is in! Yes, you can call me Dr. Lulu

Dolly Parton comes in to sing on MY album!

On stage with my pals Pam Tillis and Lorrie Morgan

I love Lorrie Morgan so much!

With Buddy Jewell

I love, love, love Randy Travis!

Moe Bandy always has a smile!

And they thought Tanya Tucker was wild...until they read MY book!

With Ricky Skaggs

Backstage with Jimmy Fortune

With Steve Hall and Shotgun Red. Steve passed away as I was finishing up my book

Jan Howard and Gus Arrendale

Oh Yeah! My pal Buck Trent

With President Carter and his wife Rosalynn

**I was so glad I was able to take Diana Goodman and her husband Roger to meet
Mr. and Mrs. Carter**

Kim, Mrs. Carter, President Carter, Lulu

I love President Jimmy Carter!

Governor Mike Huckabee

My surprise 70th birthday party. I love the look on Randy Travis' face!

Billy Dean is one of my favorite people

My buddy Mark Lowry

One of my last photos with George Lindsey. He died a short time later

Swimming with the dolphins

With Damon's father John

Nothing but smiles when I'm with Victoria Hallman and Cathy Baker

*With Misty Rowe
through the years*

Nancy Jones has been such a great friend over the years

My dear friends Leighton Nunn and Diane Curtis Fisher from Riding Point Radio have helped me in so many ways over the past couple of years. I love them very much!

Garth Brooks and his wife Trisha Yearwood always treat me so great.

Apr 23, 2015

With Kim and our great friends Norma Jean and Haskell Harris

Scot England meets me for the first time, 1987

A recent photo of Scot and me. You'll see his name on the front of this book!

What's the reaction when Aerosmith's Steven Tyler meets Hee Haw's Lulu Roman?

No, Steven Tyler was never on Hee Haw!

John Schneider, Randy Travis, Crazy Woman and Ricky Cook

Up, Up and Away!

Praising my Lord and Savior as I fly high!

I figured she was going to give me one of her favorite Bibles or something along those lines. I had to smile when I reached up in the closet and picked up a… purse! Tammy Faye whispered, "It's a Louis Vuitton. I've never used it."

I said, "I can't take this."

But like always, Tammy said, "If you don't, you'll hurt my heart."

I said, "Mine! This is mine. I will treasure it always."

I got back into bed and hugged her as I said, "You are going to dance with Jesus soon." She was gone in a week.

Tammy Faye was known to millions of people. The music of Dottie Rambo was also known around the world. Dottie wrote more than 2,500 gospel songs. But to Lulu Roman, Dottie Rambo was in the top two or three, as far as giving me spiritual guidance through my life.

Dottie Rambo was the sweetest, most honest person in the world. She was very refined. She always knew what she wanted to say. She never opened her mouth unless she knew exactly what to say, and how she was going to say it. And every time she talked, you wanted to listen.

I met Dottie in the early 70s. I had come to her house with some friends. She fixed red beans and cornbread for all of us, and for her husband Buck and young daughter Reba. Dottie was barefooted in the kitchen as she cooked the red beans, and she sang as she cooked.

I recorded a lot of her songs over the years. I sang her song "Glory in the Cross", and she paid me a great compliment, saying, "You sing that song better than I did."

I responded, "Darling, you will go to Hell for lying! No one can sing as good as you."

She was the one who taught me how to get in the throne room with God. You have to throw off everything that the world or other people have put on you. You have to get into a place where your mind is totally free of anything that this earth has. You have to be able to just listen. Dottie taught me how to be quiet and listen. You get caught up in all the junk of this world, and you miss so much that God has for you.

Dottie used to tell me all the time, "Lu, you have to get that weight off or you're going to die." After I had lost over a hundred pounds, I went and surprised Dottie. You can find the video on YouTube. She was so surprised that I was there, and she didn't even recognize me at first. When she realized it was me, she yelled, "You're gonna to live!" She was such a sweetheart.

If there ever was a mother figure in my life, it was Dottie. And even though she was just a little older than me, she taught me a lot. She taught me to keep my mouth shut when I needed to. I loved Dottie.

In the spring of 2008, Dottie, Naomi Sego and I decided to do a tour together. We called ourselves "The Golden Girls of Gospel". Our first two shows brought down the house. Everyone loved us. Our third show was scheduled for the Fountain of Life Church in North Richland Hills, Texas on Mother's Day.

We had talked about us all traveling in one bus together, but for the first few shows we did, we just traveled on our own, and would meet at each church or venue.

Naomi and I arrived in North Richland Hills, a suburb of Dallas, the night before our show. But Dottie had a show at a church in Granite City, Illinois. She told us that they would drive all night afterwards, and she'd meet us at the church in Texas.

My phone rang at 3:00 AM. The person calling told me that Dottie's bus had been involved in an accident. Her tour bus had run off the road on Interstate 44, near Mount Vernon, Missouri. I thought it was a prank call. But for the next two hours, I stayed up and prayed for my friend. At about 5:00, I got another call, and they told me that Dottie had died.

We were just a few hours from our scheduled performance, but somehow Naomi and I went ahead and did it. I know I was in a daze the entire time. I was heartbroken. We put three chairs in the middle of the stage. Naomi sat in one, and I sat in one, and we left the middle chair empty. Pastor Randy Thomas and the church staff brought flowers, and covered Dottie's chair with them.

With all my years in the orphanage, I was never a big fan of Mother's Day… but Mother's Day 2008 is one that I will never forget. I don't know how we did that concert. But I do know that God got me through it.

And only God will be able to get me through this next chapter that you are about to read.

JUSTIN

I've now come to the chapter that I have put off writing. I'm sure you will read it much faster than I wrote it. It's taken me a year to even be able to attempt it. Have you ever tried to type or write a letter while you were crying your eyes out? Hopefully my words will make sense through all my tears.

My youngest son, Justin, is gone.

OK. That's enough for today. I'll come back tomorrow.

My youngest son Justin is gone.

Maybe we can go back and talk about Hee Haw some more. That Junior Samples was so silly!

OK. I can do this.

I loved my two sons more than anything on this earth. And Justin loved his mama.

When he could, he would go with me on the road to different churches and events. When he couldn't be there, he would try to watch a live video feed through my Facebook page. As he watched, he would message me to make sure that I sang his favorite song, "He Hung the Moon".

Justin was my biggest fan. To have your own son, the person who knows you better than everyone, be your biggest fan… how cool is that? Justin always bragged to everyone that his mama was Lulu from Hee Haw. He was proud of me.

The love that Justin had for me was so precious. I can take pride in knowing that my baby loved me. He was happy with his mama. He always cheered me on, and I know that he is still cheering me on as I write this book... especially as I try to get through this chapter!

I've already talked about Justin's childhood, but now I'd like to also tell you about the man that he grew up to be.

Justin was so sweet and so tender. He was easygoing and he didn't get angry very much. He could walk up to anyone and start up a conversation with them. He was so smart. He also had a lot of wisdom about the word of God. He knew the Bible. Justin loved to debate scripture. You didn't try to tell him what the word of God said, if you didn't know the Bible very well. He'd quickly correct you if you had something wrong!

Justin worked for the state for 12 years, and everyone loved him. He worked with homeless and welfare people. He helped people get money for food. He was great with people. He was just a delightful human being.

Justin had a great voice. He loved to sing, but he didn't aspire to be a singer. And he was funny. He loved to make people laugh. He was like his mama there. Justin was also a lot like me, in that he loved food! Oh my God, he loved to eat, and he grew to be a huge man. His being so overweight was always a concern. He also smoked.

He owned and operated a food truck, which he named "Bacon Nation". He loved bacon. Justin also loved swords and sci-fi stuff. He liked to play video games, and he loved Marvel Comics. He also loved going to the Comic Conventions. One of the highlights of his life is when he got his photo with Stan Lee, the man who created all the Marvel superheroes.

On October 29, 2017, my assistant Kim and I were driving home after a performance in Branson, Missouri. My cell phone rang, and it was Justin's roommate Cory. He told me that I needed to get to the hospital in Nashville as fast as I could, because Justin had suffered a major heart attack.

Cory told me that Justin had been home, and had gone outside to smoke a cigarette, and then he just collapsed. We never had any warning that anything was wrong with him. Cory called an ambulance, and they took him to the hospital.

Kim drove as fast as she could to get me to Justin. But when I got there, they told me he was gone. But he wasn't. I went into his room, took his hand and said, "Baby, please come back to me." Justin opened his eyes. He knew I had made it there. But he never said anything. I told him that I loved him. I stayed with him until he died.

Justin was 41 years old.

To lose a child… it is the deepest wound that you can ever have.

I still hear his voice. When I think about him, I can still hear his voice. He was such a great kid.

My spirit was so low and so wounded when Justin died. I got mad at God. God had let my son die, and I was crushed. I'd never felt pain like that in my life. It's just not right that a mother loses a child. It's just not. And there is nothing that anyone can say, there is nothing that anyone can do. It's all on you… and God.

After Justin died, Damon came home and spent a month with me. He helped clean out Justin's closets and things. I went with him to Justin's house, and as we were going through some of his things, I found the photo of him with Stan Lee. Justin was so thrilled to meet him. He had such a big smile in the picture. I thought, "I know that Justin is smiling even bigger because now he is in the presence of Jesus." I'm sure he is. I know he is having a big time with Jesus right now. But I miss him so much.

I had to cancel all my appearances for a month or so after Justin died. I couldn't go out, because I would just break down. During the first few shows I did after his death, I broke down while I was singing. But everyone completely understood. After pulling myself together, I was able to finish my show.

When your heart is completely broken, and you want to cry all the time, it is not real easy to go out and make a crowd of people laugh... but I know Justin would want me to go on. So we started booking a few more shows. Once I got into my testimony, however, I didn't bring up my son's death. I stopped talking about it. I just couldn't do it. I went back to my original testimony, from before he had died.

Now, there are some songs I can't sing anymore. I don't know if I'll ever be able to sing "He Hung the Moon" again in public. That was Justin's favorite. He always asked me to sing it. So if you see me in a church somewhere, and I sing it, you will know that my healing has continued. I hope you get to hear me sing it one day.

In the first year after Justin's death, I would go out to the cemetery and just lay down on his grave. You don't ever think it's possible for your child to die before you. When it happens, you don't know how it's possible that you can go on.

The only thing that gave me hope, and kept me going, was knowing that my son knew Jesus.

I really do feel like my story could help people. I do. But right now, I honestly don't know how it could help 'em, other than them saying, "Oh my God, she has been through what I am going through." For anyone who is going through something like that, I would like to say that there is hope when you put your trust in the Lord. There is hope, and you can do this.

But you can lose that hope, if you allow the enemy to stab your spirit so deeply that you get mad at God. If you do that, you can feel that hope has been taken. I have been there. When Justin died, I felt hopeless.

I have to be honest with you. In the year after Justin died, I was angry at God. I didn't want to be, but I couldn't help it. My heart was in turmoil. I was mad!

But I have tried to let go of that, as I struggled to try to trust God again with my lonely heart.

I had to deal with selling Justin's house, and taking care of all of his stuff. Going on without my son is the hardest thing I've ever done. There are days when I can hardly get out of bed. I just lay there and cry. But I know that I will see Justin again in Heaven. I have no doubt whatsoever.

I was told in the very beginning of my Christian walk that I was going to suffer. The louder I proclaimed the word of Jesus to the world, the more I would suffer. Dear God, have I suffered. God allowed my child to suddenly drop dead at the age of just 41. The first thing that came to my mind when I heard that Justin had died was, "Oh great God. I am an orphan and now you took my child." I don't believe in my spirit that God took my child. I really don't. I know that the Devil had a hand in that.

I know that my baby was like me, he was a rebel. Both of my children are, and both of my sons loved Jesus. I think the most important thing you can do in your life is get your children to Jesus. My boys loved Jesus, and they loved their mama.

I have been "proclaiming the love of Jesus" for the past 45 years. Without a doubt, I can tell you that a person does not stand up and wear the name of Jesus in public without the Devil raging war on them.

A lot of people don't believe in Hell or the Devil. But I will tell you this, the Devil is real. And he has tried to kill me every day. He almost got it done in 2017 when my son died. But guess what... the Devil failed! Instead of taking a bunch of pills and dying, guess what

Lulu Roman did? She spent all year writing a book of her life story, and she lifted up Jesus louder than she ever had before!

If you've gone through a similar year, you need to know that there is hope. Life is not easy. You have to fight. There will still be pain. I'll never get over the pain of losing Justin. But you have to go on. You can't let the Devil destroy your life. Let this be the year that you tell Satan to go to Hell.

There you go Justin, my son. I got through your chapter.

Telling funny stories about Junior Samples would have been a lot easier.

LOVING LULU

I have been blessed to receive quite a few awards and honors in my career, with many even coming over the past few years.

In 1985, I won a Dove Award when my "When You Were Loving Me" album was named Best Album by a Secular Artist. That year, I also had a number one song with a duet with Russ Taff called, "King of Who I Am". When the radio stations started playing the song, they kept my identity a secret, and my record label had a contest to see if people could guess who I was. A couple years later, I hit the top of the charts again, when I teamed up with Ricky Skaggs and Sharon White on a song called "Two More Hands".

In 1999, I was inducted into the Country Gospel Music Hall of Fame. Andy Griffith, Barbara Mandrell and Loretta Lynn were also inducted into the Hall of Fame that same year. In 2008, I won the Diamond Award and the J.D. Sumner Living Legend Award. That same year, I was also inducted into the Christian Music Hall of Fame.

One honor that I will never forget came when I was invited back to the orphanage where I had spent 15 years of my life. They'd asked me to give my testimony for the church service during their 1994 Homecoming Weekend. 30 years had passed since I had called that place home, but it seemed like it was just yesterday.

When I returned for the reunion, hundreds of memories all came back to me, some of them good, but some of them very bad. It was hard. I remembered things I thought I had hidden away forever. In all of those memories, I could not recall even one time that someone had ever held me when I was a child. I remembered how I never had a bicycle. I never had a doll… with the exception of that embarrassing giant thing that my "mom" gave me when I was about to graduate high school!

But please do not send me dolls! I was once on one of the Bill Gaither specials, and I mentioned that I'd never had a doll when I was a little girl, and people started sending me dolls by the hundreds! I finally had to fill up my garage with all the dolls people gave me.

When I gave my testimony at the Buckner Baptist Children's Home Homecoming Weekend, I gave them my ENTIRE testimony. I told it all! I told them how I was treated back then, and how hurt I was. Afterward, three women came up to me. Many years earlier, they had been three girls who'd all treated me very badly when I was little, and one of them was the girl who was the absolute meanest to me.

When we met again, she got down on her knees and begged me to forgive her. She put her head on my lap and just wept. Of course I did too. It was awesome. For them to repent and say they were sorry, it was so freeing for them and for me. That was the day that God finished breaking the chains that had kept me tied to that place for my entire life.

My favorite scripture is Jeremiah 29:11-14. "For I know the plans that I have for you, plans to prosper you and not to harm you, but plans to give you hope and a future. If you will seek my face with all your heart, I will be found by you, and I will ultimately lead you out of the bondage."

That is exactly what the Lord did for me. He delivered me from bondage.

In the fall of 2016, I was honored when President Jimmy Carter requested that I come to Plains, Georgia to do a Saturday night concert at his church. It was hard to believe that 40 years had passed since I had been elected as a delegate to help Jimmy Carter win the Democratic nomination for President of the United States.

After my concert in President Carter's church, we talked for an hour, and then he asked me to sing during the church service the next morning.

Before the service, the security officials told everyone, "When you are getting a photo with the President, DO NOT touch him! Do not try to put your arm around him for your picture!"

But as soon as I walked up to Mr. Carter, he grabbed my hand. He started hugging me and holding onto me. He patted me on the back, and then gave me a kiss!

Jimmy Carter was so precious. He is a true man of God. He was so sweet, and he is really a southern gentleman. I took my assistant Kim with me. I also took Hee Haw Honey Diana Goodman, and her husband Roger. Roger died just a year later. I was so glad that I'd gotten to introduce them to President Carter.

Ironically, I also performed at President Reagan's inauguration. On January 19, 1980, I sang at the "First Annual Christian Inauguration Celebration". It was held at the National Guard Armory, and included Sandi Patty, Larnelle Harris and some other folks. There, I sang "Amazing Grace" for President Reagan.

A very unexpected honor came in the small town of Haleyville, Alabama. I was invited to perform at a women's conference there in December of 1998, and at the end of my show, they brought a big Christmas present on stage. When I opened it, I burst into tears. The town of Haleyville was officially adopting me! I cried and cried, and then I cried some more… all tears of joy.

It was a very special thing. Nobody had ever made any kind of gesture like that for me before. The mayor came, and gave me an official adoption certificate. Everyone from the whole town showed up, and it was really precious. I have been given lots of keys to the city from places I've played, but I've never heard of a town actually adopting someone. I will always be proud to say that I am an adopted child of Haleyville, Alabama.

Ten years later, I became a member of another family. Earl Hamner, Jr. was the writer and producer of the TV show "The Waltons". Earl also became well-known as the narrator of the show. Earl grew up in the Blue Ridge Mountains of Virginia, and he'd based "The Waltons" on his own family and childhood.

On October 4, 2008, I was doing a benefit concert to raise money for an Alzheimer's organization. During the event, I was surprised and very touched when Earl Hamner presented me with a framed proclamation he had written. It reads: "Because of her love for her fellow human beings, because of her efforts to alleviate pain and suffering, because of her love of God and country, because she has brought us laughter and lifted our hearts with her songs, as the senior member of the clan, it's my greatest pleasure to declare Lulu Roman an honorary member of the Walton family."

Being a member of The Waltons was quite an honor, and when I was 70 years old, my family grew even more. I got an email from a man, who said, "I think I am kin to you." I've heard that quite a few times over the years, but it never turned out to be true. But this time, when the gentleman mentioned my original family name, I thought that maybe there was something to it.

A short time later, I was doing a show in Texas, and that couple came to meet me. As soon as they walked up, I recognized his nose! It was the same as mine. Their names were Daris and Judy Hable. They were cousins that I never knew I had. Their two boys look like my boys. Daris and Judy are the same age as me, and we got to know each other for the first time when we were in our 70s.

OLD FRIENDS... AND A NEW DAUGHTER

I have recorded quite a few albums over the years, and one of my favorite songwriters is Michael Wells. Michael has written some of my best songs, including "Heaven's Watchin'" and "When I Don't Call Your Name". I met Michael almost twenty years ago, and we became great friends almost instantly. He stayed in a spare room that I had for a few months. We liked to sit on the porch and sing one gospel song after another.

During one of those evenings, Michael told me that when he was eight years old, his parents were watching "Hee Haw" on TV. He'd seen me singing "Blessed Assurance", and at that moment, the Lord had told him that he would work with me one day. He was just a little boy! And now, almost thirty years later, here he was, writing songs for me! Yes, God works in mysterious ways. God will put his hand on you and direct you where he wants you to go, if you will allow it.

In 1991, I was signed to the Benson Company. It was one of the biggest record labels in gospel music. Norman Holland was the man who signed me to the label. Norman stood almost seven foot tall, but his reputation in the southern gospel industry was even bigger. He was the very best. Everyone wanted to work with him, and Norman wanted to work with Lulu Roman!

Norman Holland was one of my biggest fans, and one of my biggest supporters. His support continued when he became Vice President of Daywind Records. Norman did everything he could do to keep me in the public eye. In April of 2001, Norman went with me, as I taped one of Bill Gaither's Homecoming Specials in Alexandria,

Indiana. My friend Mark Lowry is the person who talked Bill into having me on the show. As we began taping, I looked around at all of the gospel music legends in the room, including Howard and Vestal Goodman, J.D. Sumner, the Cathedrals, and so many others. I knew this must be what heaven's choir looks like.

Since I had never had a family, I had also never experienced a family reunion. So the Gaither Homecoming was as close as I will probably ever come. During the show, I shared some of my story. I told them how I had never felt the love of a mother or father, or a brother or sister. When we took a break, the legendary Jake Hess walked over and put his hands on my face, as he asked, "Lulu, could I be your big brother?"

Then J.D. Sumner and George Younce both came over, and said they would be my brothers. I was totally speechless.

I will be forever grateful to Bill and Gloria Gaither, for allowing me to be a part of that incredible experience. I'm so glad that Norman Holland was able to enjoy the Homecoming taping with me. He had helped many of the artists who were in the room, but he helped no one more than me. Norman believed in me when I didn't believe in myself. He stuck by me through the good times and the bad times, and he was truly one of the closest friends that I've ever had in my life. I was heartbroken when Norman died of heart failure in March of 2014. He was just 54 years old.

I've been blessed to try many different styles in the studio. Of course, I started out singing gospel music. Singing for the Lord is the reason I sing at all. But I've also sung country, jazz, and even bluegrass.

I did a bluegrass album with a group called "Chosen Road" a few years ago. "Chosen Road" is a group of young Christian men. And over the past few years, they became like my own children.

When we were looking for songs to record, I saw Ricky Skaggs on a TV show, doing a song called "Cluck Ol' Hen". As a joke, I suggested that we do the song, but "Chosen Road" thought it was a great idea. I ended up writing a new verse to the song. It includes a reference to Springer Mountain Farms chicken, and I dedicated the song to Gus Arrendale, the President of the Springer Mountain Farms. Gus has done so much for country music, and has always been a big supporter of everything I do. I love him very much.

The day after we'd finished recording the "Heavenly Heartstrings" album, Jonathan Buckner, the leader of "Chosen Road", adopted a little girl. Of course, after all those years I had spent in that orphan's home, that meant so much to me.

In 2013, I did an album called "At Last". Out of all of the albums I've done, it is by far the very best one I have ever recorded. "At Last" is the album I am most proud of. It's an album of old classics and standards, and I loved them all.

I really put my heart and soul into the "At Last" album. I sang "Precious Lord, Take My Hand", a song I had heard when I first started doing gospel music. When I heard Mahalia Jackson singing "Precious Lord", I knew it was something very special, and I always wanted to do it. I was always into rhythm and blues, and I always loved soulful music. So I tried to find soulful gospel music.

I heard the Joe Cocker song, "You are so Beautiful", and I have said for many, many years, "That should be a gospel song to Jesus." I found out that Billy Preston and Bruce Fisher had originally written the song to be a gospel song, and I sing it as a love song to Jesus. I sing it in almost every appearance that I do.

But on the "At Last" album, I sang it as a duet with T. Graham Brown. Linda Davis and I also sang "You Needed Me" as a duet, and Georgette Jones, the daughter of George Jones and Tammy Wynette, joined me on "Till I Can Make It on My Own", the song her mama had a big hit with.

One of the songs that got the most attention on that album was one that I did with Dolly Parton. We did her classic "I Will Always Love You" as a duet. We were both in the studio together, and when I started singing, Dolly exclaimed, "Lulu, I had no idea you could sing like that!"

"At Last" really is a great album. You can buy one when you come see me, when I come sing somewhere near you! When you do that, the person who will sell you a copy is named Kim. Kim is my assistant, and she also runs my music and sells my CDs and photos. Kim is my driver, and she also books all of my appearances and makes sure that we get to each one on time. She takes good care of my scheduling, hotels and travel.

I've always loved to travel, and when I first started touring with my gospel music, I would travel by myself. I didn't mind jumping on a plane alone and going to my next event. But as I got older, I found that I wanted some company.

Kim is the daughter I never had. She is one of the greatest gifts the Lord has given me in my life. She is a couple decades younger than me, but she has become my mother! She protects me physically and emotionally. She is the most dedicated, loyal and hardworking person. She is a rock in my life. She takes care of everything for me, all of my business and personal needs.

I stole Kim from Jim Bakker ten years ago. She had been working with Jim in Branson at the time. I went up to do his show several times, and on one of my visits there, Kim stayed with me for a week, and made sure that I got everywhere I needed to be. We got to know each other, and I saw how great she was.

I always saw Kim working so hard there, but it seemed like the harder and faster she worked, the more people were yelling orders at her. I told her that she wasn't being appreciated at her job like she should be. She was so dedicated. A short time later, she left Jim and said that she was available if I needed a personal assistant. I told her she would find out I didn't live a life of luxury!

Since my kids were grown and off making their own lives, Kim came in and has just been God's gift to my life. She takes such great care to do everything she can to make me comfortable, safe and loved. She brings me a cup of hot coffee or coco every morning. She has a great heart, and is so humble.

Kim will be with me until I die. She is very precious. She has committed her life to taking care of me. I can still take care of myself, but it's always nice to have someone to talk to, and someone to help you with things. God really sent me an angel when I found her.

I know that God also sent me my dear friends Dianne Brady and Rhonda Hanson. They have also been really great spiritual leaders for me. Rhonda covers me in prayer every day. I love her so much. She was from Louisiana, but we met when she came to visit my church. She and I just hit it off instantly, and we sat up talking for hours and hours. We have been great friends ever since. I love her so much. She is one of my dearest friends in all the world. Rhonda and her husband, Val, are my prayer warriors, and I am so thankful for them.

UP, UP AND AWAY!

Today, when I'm not singing on a stage or in a church, there is one place that you can usually find me… but you'll have to look up… way up! I love to zipline! I would zipline every day of my life if I had time. I'd do it ten times a day if I could. It is so much fun. I praise the Lord the entire way across. I raise my hands and sing all the way.

I love to zipline at the Shepard of the Hills in Branson, Missouri. They treat me so good at the Shepard of the Hills. They never charge me, and if I want to zipline ten times in a row, they'll just let me go. They are just so awesome. I get up there and I spread my arms, and just start praising the Lord and sing all the way across. I like the feel of freedom. It's like flying, and you feel like nothing can stop you as you are soaring. It's just incredible. I absolutely love it. It makes me so happy.

I've always been a daredevil. I've jumped out of airplanes. I've parachuted three times, all on my own. I have always been willing to try anything, but folks are always surprised when they see a 200-plus pound, 73 year old woman jumping out of a plane or ziplining above the trees!

But I also enjoy my quieter moments at home. When I'm sad or stressed, I like to color. I color in the books that they now make for adults. I color for hours each day. They're not like children's coloring books; most of them are very intricate. I have more than 150 coloring books, and more than 500 pencils. I color all the time.

I also love making crafts. I make jewelry, like button bracelets with crystal and glass, and they are just gorgeous. I have thousands of beads and metal pieces that I make bracelets from.

During the Christmas Season, you can probably find me in the kitchen. I love to make candy that I call "White Trash" at Christmas. It's nuts, pretzels and cereal covered in white chocolate. People go crazy over it. You can't stop eating it! I also make the best chocolate fudge. Tammy Faye Bakker loved my fudge.

As I now head toward my mid 70s, I still have a few goals left. I would like to go to Japan, and I'd like to go to Ireland. After reading about all the bad luck I've had with men, you'd probably think I have sworn off marriage. I haven't. I wouldn't be opposed to being married again. I would love to have someone in my life. But I think I might be destined to be alone, and if that's the case, I'm OK with that.

Another goal I have is that I want a kennel, to breed and care for Yorkies. I love those dogs. I guess I treat my little dogs like they're my grandchildren. I have never had grandkids. I wanted some, but it never happened. I think that if it had happened, I would have wanted to stay home with them all the time. It might have meant the end of my touring ministry.

Even at the age of 73, I don't think that God is finished with me yet. I feel like I still have a lot more to do. I believe with my whole heart that I am supposed to stand up and tell people that Jesus is real. And I do that as often as I possibly can.

Singing is still my favorite thing to do in life. Singing and eating! I hope the Lord will allow me to sing until I leave this earth. Every time I get to stand up on stage and sing, it is a very special moment for me. The joy of my life is getting to sing. It is a gift from God that I can sing, and still sing on key, today. I can still knock the walls down with my voice. I believe that that's a miracle. All the credit for that goes to

God. I want to get on my face and say thank you to Jesus every day that he lets me sing. I serve a mighty God.

A lot of artists that I knew are long gone. So many have died. The ones who are still here, if they are my age, most of them will have a little wobble in their voice, or they can't hit the notes that they used to. But I can still hit them. The fact that God still lets me sing, and still helps me to sing strong… that is a miracle. I am so blessed that I can still sing like I do.

I am very thankful for everything the Lord has allowed me to do. I am thankful for so many good times, and I'm thankful that the Lord has helped me survive through so many bad times… most of those through my own making. I am so thankful for "Hee Haw". It changed my life. It probably saved my life.

The enemy (Satan) is going to give you one thing that will mess with you your whole life. My one thing was never knowing who my father was. I never got to see my father. I never got to touch or hug my father, or have him hug me. And I've often wondered how knowing him would have changed or defined my life. When you don't know who your father is, it makes it tough for you to ever fully know who you are.

All of the previous paragraph is true. But thanks to my relationship with the Lord, none of the above matters anymore.

I know who I am in God's eyes. I know that I'm God's child. It is the greatest joy in my life to have found my Father. I do know my Father… my heavenly Father. He has watched over me, and protected me, through my entire life. I can't wait to get the biggest, tightest hug ever given from him the moment I walk into Heaven. And I pray that I hear God say, "Well done, my good and faithful servant."

PARTING SONG

I met Lulu Roman for the first time in June of 1987. If we had started this book back then, it would have been finished four decades ago! But Lulu Roman had a lot of living to do over the last forty years.

During that time, Lulu has brought smiles and laughter to millions of people, and she has also brought thousands to tears with her testimony. And more importantly, she has brought countless people to the Lord.

I was always a fan of Hee Haw and Lulu Roman. Like so many others, I was thrilled when I met her in person. But even back in 1987, I could feel that there was something different about Lulu. There was something that drew me to her.

Over the past four decades, I've said hello to Lulu at least once a year, usually at Fan Fair in Nashville. A few years ago, I did a TV interview with her. It was supposed to be a simple ad for an upcoming event she was promoting , but it quickly turned into an in-depth and quite amazing interview. Our short Q&A session went on for more than an hour, and at the end of that time, Lulu said, "I have never been asked questions like that." Then she asked if I would help her write her autobiography.

While I was sincerely honored, I told her that I was much too busy. A couple years later, I ran into Lulu again, and again, she asked if I would help her with her book. I explained that my workload had tripled since I had first told her I was too busy. But then, I found myself saying, "Lulu, you know that I love you, and there is something about you that I just cannot say 'No' to. I will find the time to do it."

Over the last year, as we've worked on this book, I have finally figured out what it was that kept drawing me to her. I now know why I had always felt true joy when I was around her. I was seeing Jesus in Lulu.

Lulu Roman is real. She is honest. If you have read her book this far, you already know that she is real honest! She is saved. But she still struggles with all of the issues that we all face in life. She laughs louder than anyone I've ever met, and she cries more than anyone I've ever met. If you want to be a part of tears and laughter on a daily basis... spend a day, any day, with Lulu Roman.

She has been willing to share her darkest moments, in an effort to help keep someone else from going through the things that she has. And she has been willing to share her testimony, in an effort to make sure that YOU are going to the same place she is, when YOUR life story on this earth is done.

Thank you for allowing me to help you tell your story, Lu. I love you so much. I'll see you on the zipline very soon.

– Scot England